Cooking with Passion

THE BEST FROM CONSUMING PASSIONS
IAN PARMENTER

ABC
BOOKS

Contents

Published by ABC Books for the
AUSTRALIAN BROADCASTING CORPORATION
GPO Box 9994 Sydney NSW 2001

Copyright © Ian Parmenter 1999

First published 1999

ISBN 0 7333 0800 7

Editorial package: Media21
Managing Editor: Philip Gore
Design: Sharon McGrath
Illustrations: Ian Parmenter
Researcher: Ann Dewar
Cover photograph: Frances Andrijich
Food photography: Joe Filshie
Styling: Georgina Dolling
Home Economist: Christine Sheppard
Editor: Loukie Werle
Thanks to Accoutrement
Colour separations by Setrite, Hong Kong
Printed in China by Everbest

5 4 3 2 1

Foreword

Food and wine are my universe, my night and my day, my Pavarotti and Sting, my heaven on a stick.

My first memory involved food. A clumsy, hungry toddler, I had just fallen down the stairs of our London house. As I lay there, battered and bruised, awaiting urgent parental attention, I remember noticing the enticing aroma of rhubarb pie baking in the kitchen and knew that, after she had attended to my wounds, my mother would be sprinkling caster sugar over the pie's golden top and serving it to me with a smooth, thick, hot custard made properly with egg yolks, vanilla essence and full cream milk.

My earliest and greatest childhood disappointment – in those pre-lunar landing days – was to learn that the moon was not in fact made of cheese. You see, I intended to be an astronaut and had cheese board, knife and cream crackers packed. (In the end NASA beat me to it and I became a gastronaut instead!)

Cuisine in Britain at that time was pretty lean. There wasn't much fat either, though we did consume copious quantities of such delights as lard and camp pie, thanks to the food parcels generously sent from Australia, and for which we were grateful. The old saying that 'the English have three vegetables, two of which are cabbage', seemed to hold true.

I was rather glad when, one Tuesday, my parents carted me off to Brussels and a new life brim full of such wonders as the Belgian national dish of twice-cooked chips and mayonnaise, pork cooked with prunes, chicken prepared in a lemon and cream sauce, waffles covered with thick cream, and Belgian chocolates. (I don't remember ever seeing a brussels sprout in Brussels.)

I never looked back across the Channel. Well, eventually I did when I was exiled from this gastronomic paradise and sent to purgatory in the form of an old British boarding school. The second oldest in England, it was founded by Bishop Gundulf in 604 AD (truly) and re-founded by Henry VIII in 1542 (I still wonder how you can re-found something). I was convinced this King's School had the original plumbing and kitchen staff.

It was there, in Rochester, Kent – the city famous for having had Charles Dickens – that we schoolboys were fed a diet which would have made Oliver Twist think twice about asking for more.

For instance, one of the school kitchen's specialities was tinned pilchards in tomato sauce, warmed at three in the afternoon, placed on toast and allowed to stand for three hours before it was served for tea. Not a good look, nor taste sensation, nor texture come to that.

Despite the school dinners, I grew up and, as soon as I could, grabbed my Elizabeth David 'French Provincial Cooking' and the Larousse Gastronomique and fled to Australia, the land of the barbecue, where happily I have lived ever since.

My first 17 years in Oz were spent producing and directing TV shows for the ABC. All went perfectly well until one day in 1991 when I was hurled screaming and kicking in front of a television camera. I was ordered by no less a person than the Big Cheese of ABC Television to make a cooking series of 45 programmes. And I have not been the same since. It was a case of out of the televisual frying pan and into the fire.

The rest – as they say – is history. I started with 15 recipes in my repertoire and now, into my ninth year of *Consuming Passions* on ABCTV, I'm approaching the 400 mark. Though I've prepared most of the dishes in my own Fremantle kitchen, I've also been privileged to watch the country's great chefs – and they're among the world's best – cook in theirs, and I've met some of the nation's most dedicated food, wine and beer producers, educators and writers.

Eight years on I realise I'm still only skimming the surface of the fascinating subject of food. But if I've learned anything along the way, it's that most of us don't just eat to live. We love to eat. And we love preparing food for others. As George Bernard Shaw put it in Man and Superman: 'There is no love sincerer than the love of food'.

This book is a celebration of my love of food and cooking, providing many of my favourite recipes, along with a miscellany of anecdotes, some handy hints, and some of my scribblings to fill in the gaps.

I hope you find it entertaining as well as informative. And remember that, as US writer Fran Lebowitz once put it: 'If food did not exist it would be well-nigh impossible to get certain types off the phone.'

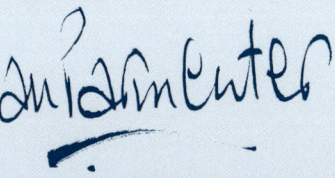

Dedication...

To Ann
To my parents, Billie and Paul, for building the foundation for a rich culinary life

Acknowledgments...

My thanks to all those who have contributed to the continuing success of 'Consuming Passions'. To Paddy Conroy and Michael Shrimpton for having the foresight to hurl me in front of the camera in 1991.

To the ABCTV directors – especially Kevin Firkins and David de Vos – and the camera crews around the country whose work has contributed to almost 400 episodes of the TV series. To Jane Dewar and Anna Gare for their help behind the scenes.

To my colleagues and friends at 'Consuming Passions': Executive Producer David Evans, Marina Libia, Annette Libia and Michael Buffham for their constant support, hard work and good humour. To Maree Curtis, Jill Baker and Garry (Dolmio Kid) Linnell, my former editors at 'The Sunday Age', where much of this book's text originally appeared.

To the many chefs, apprentices, food producers, wine makers, brewers, food writers and educators, hoteliers and restaurateurs, who have so willingly shared their knowledge over the years.

To Philip Gore, Craig Osment, Sue Short and Stephen Balme for their contributions to this book. To Frances Andrijich and Joe Filshie for their photographs, and to Georgina Dolling for her food styling.

To ABC publisher Matthew Kelly for his enthusiasm throughout the project.

Above all to my partner, Ann Dewar, who works closely with me on the TV shows and publications, keeps my life in perspective, has the best one-liners, and always knows where I've put things.

"It isn't so much what's on the table that matters, as what's on the chairs"

W. S. GILBERT

Beginnings

Spinach and Chick Pea Soup

A thoroughly healthy and nourishing soup with just a hint of spice.

Serves 4

INGREDIENTS

200g chick peas, soaked in
  water overnight
2 onion quarters
2 or 3 cloves
2 bay leaves
1 head of garlic (yes, that's a
  lot of cloves of garlic!),
  loose dry outer skin
  removed
500g fresh spinach
1 tsp sesame oil
1 tbsp extra virgin olive oil
2 cloves garlic, finely chopped
2 tbsp freshly made
  breadcrumbs
3 tbsp chopped parsley
2 tbsp chopped coriander
  leaves and/or
½ tsp ground coriander
1 tsp chilli sauce (optional)

To serve cold

1 tbsp finely diced tomato
  flesh
1 tbsp finely diced capsicum
1 tbsp finely diced lebanese
  cucumber

METHOD

Drain chick peas. Put in a large saucepan and cover with water. Stud onion quarters with cloves. Add onion, bay leaves and the whole head of garlic to the pan.

Simmer very slowly for 1 hour or so until the chick peas are cooked – they should still be firm, but not crunchy.

Meanwhile, strip the spinach leaves from the stalks. Wash and drain, but not too thoroughly – some water may remain on the leaves.

In a large saucepan, gently cook spinach leaves in the sesame oil for about 1 minute or until they wilt. Remove spinach from pan.

Add the olive oil, finely chopped garlic, breadcrumbs and parsley to the pan and cook for 2-3 minutes.

Crush garlic/bread mixture to a pulp with 2-3 tsp of the cooking water from the chick peas. Set aside.

When the chick peas are cooked, remove the head of garlic and onion segments. Squeeze garlic paste from the cooked garlic.

Add garlic paste, spinach, bread mixture to chick peas and cooking water. Add coriander and chili sauce (if using) and season to taste before serving. Reheat if serving hot.

To serve cold: Chill soup. Serve soup garnished with diced tomato, capsicum and cucumber.

Leftover potential: The soup keeps for two or three days in the refrigerator.

Cheese and Pecan Crackers

An ideal appetiser which may be served on special occasions with champagne. These are light, spicy and buttery, cheesy biscuits.

Makes about 15-20 biscuits

INGREDIENTS
100g unsalted butter
100g plain flour
100g grated cheese
$1/4$ tsp nutmeg
1 egg, beaten
50g pecan nuts, finely chopped
sprinkling of pepper to taste

METHOD
Cut the butter into small cubes and rub into the flour.

Add the grated cheese and nutmeg. Knead into a paste.

Roll out thinly and cut into preferred shapes with a sharp knife or pastry cutter. Brush each biscuit shape with the beaten egg. Then sprinkle with the chopped pecan nuts and bake on a large baking tray, covered with baking paper at 180°C for 10 minutes or until golden.

Rice Paper Rolls

A delightful snack or a light lunch, rice paper rolls require no cooking and are simply splendid served cold with a dipping sauce.

Serves 6

INGREDIENTS

100g cooked prawn flesh
100g cooked crab meat
1 cup finely shredded cos
  lettuce
1 cup chopped bean sprouts
6 or 7 water chestnuts, finely
  chopped
2 tbsp finely chopped
  Vietnamese mint or basil
2 tbsp finely chopped
  coriander leaves,
1/2 tsp cracked black pepper
1/4 tsp five spice
2 tsp sesame oil
1 cup rice vermicelli, softened
  in hot water first
salt to taste
6 chives (or strips of spring
  onion)
12 rice paper sheets (or 1 pkt)

Dipping sauce

2 tbsp hoisin sauce
2 tsp soy sauce
1 tsp sesame oil
1 tsp chilli sauce (or more,
  to taste)
2 tbsp chopped peanuts
  (garnish on the side)

METHOD

To make the rolls: Chop the prawns and crab meat and mix them with all other ingredients, except the chives and rice paper sheets. Add some salt to taste.

Dunk a rice paper sheet in very hot water for a few seconds to soften (they shouldn't need cooking). Drain on a damp tea towel.

Put a dollop of the mixture on the leading edge, leaving enough room to fold it over the mixture. Fold the sides over the mixture. Insert a chive, leaving the end sticking out (like a small handle). Roll up and store under a damp towel until ready to use. Repeat with rice paper sheets until all the mixture is used.

To make the dipping sauce: Mix all the ingredients (except the peanuts) together in a small serving bowl.

Serving suggestion: To eat, dunk the rice paper roll in the dipping sauce, then dunk in the peanuts and eat.

Leftover potential: Best eaten soon after making as they can dry out. May be stored for a couple of hours under plastic cling wrap in the refrigerator.

Wine choice: A crisp cold Sauvignon Blanc is ideal.

Scottish Broth

A Consuming Passions version of a classic Scottish soup using mutton meat and bones, vegetables, herbs and pearl barley. This version was put to the test by the boys of the Scotch College pipe band in Perth, Western Australia. It easily passed the test!

Serves 6

INGREDIENTS

2kg mutton neck and/or
  shanks
3 onions, roughly chopped
2 large parsnip, roughly
  chopped
2 or 3 carrots, diced
2 large leeks, cut into rings
2 sticks celery, chopped
2 bay leaves
20 or so peppercorns
3 tbsp pearl barley
1 tbsp chopped parsley

METHOD

Put the mutton/shanks into a large saucepan and cover with water. Bring to the boil.

Once the water has been boiling for about five or six minutes, skim the surface, removing any floating matter.

Add all the onion, two-thirds of the other vegetables, the bay leaves and the peppercorns.

Reduce the heat and allow to simmer for 3 hours, very, very slowly.

Remove the fat, either by spooning it out and then using a kitchen paper towel, or by refrigerating the soup overnight and removing the cold fat sitting on the top the following day, which is much easier.

Warm the soup and strain, reserving the mutton bones and the meat.

Put the strained liquid back into the pan, along with the remaining vegetables and the pearl barley.

Simmer for 45 minutes, or until the pearl barley is cooked. Remove the meat from the bones.

Before serving, stir the meat through the soup then add the parsley and lemon rind, and season to taste.

Comfort Zone

It's swoon food. Nostalgic food. Slow food. Food that belongs with big Beethoven symphonies – unlike fast food which goes better with Kenny Gee.

Sitting in a hot bath with a bowl of piping hot macaroni cheese and a glass of gut-scouring Spanish red on the side was paradise. At least that's what I thought when I was a poverty strapped 20-something journalist living in an ice-box of a London flat in the '60s.

So cold was it that I would spend my evenings in the bath, mostly listening to conversations from the basement through the holes in the floor, beneath which the four female haematologists would argue about blood cells and boyfriends .

It was a way of being comfortable, without and within, in the depths of an English winter, where the only appetite bigger than mine belonged to the gas meter, which happily gobbled up the shillings required to run the largely ineffectual fire – which was hot only if you touched it.

Apart from the bath, the only other place to avoid being frozen solid would have been the fridge, also largely ineffectual but where at least there were no draughts. However, it was too small to accommodate me.

So cold were those days – and nights – that I would put my clothes in the oven at a low setting for 20 minutes each morning before putting them on my shivering body, and setting off for work in the City.

Food therefore was vital both for fuel and comfort. It was in those days that nutritious soups, steak and kidney puddings, and roast

Memories of England in the '60s, where the only appetite bigger than mine belonged to the gas meter.

dinners – when meat could be afforded – were the order of the day, along with mountains of potatoes, root vegetables and pasta. Cauliflower cheese, shepherd's pie, and canned ravioli in tomato sauce made regular appearances on the menu.

Eating out was invariably done in pubs (macaroni cheese, sausage and mash) or in cheap Italian or Greek restaurants, where a slab of lasagna or a dish of moussaka would be gobbled down before going to the 'pictures', another source of heat, cinemas always being hotter than anywhere else.

Here the custom was to take along that comfort confectionery, halva, the sesame and honey flavoured sweet with its crumbly asbestos texture, most of which would end up glued to one's clothing.

And now, more than a quarter of a century later, after cuisine nouvelle and the dietary zealotry of recent times has been eased on to the back burner, it seems that comfort foods are making a welcome return to our lives.

Of the thousands of requests which come in each week for the Consuming Passions television recipes, the majority are for those dishes that many of us grew up with. Consumers are looking to go back to basics, to real food, stuff that nurtures or as it was once described: 'food that sticks to your ribs'. Casseroles using cheaper meat cuts, thick wholesome soups made from scratch, and steamed puddings have found their way back into our kitchens, on to restaurant menus and into our hearts (metaphorically speaking).

Scrambled eggs, creamy seafood bisques, and crèmes brûlés need not be the forbidden fruits they once were, if eaten sensibly.

And once in a while don't we all need the nurturing provided by comfort foods? Heaven help us if we follow the trend from America that would have us breakfasting on scrambled egg whites and 'decaf skinny-cinos'.

What makes a food comfort-giving? Isn't it that it's more or less grown-up baby food? Dishes that are easy to eat, that pose no threat to the chew-challenged, that aren't too spicy or too sharp, that don't have too many contrasting flavours or textures – and that aren't too salty or too sweet.

For me it's the chicken soup served up when one is ailing – actually made with chicken – or poached fish fillets with smooth parsley sauce on a bed of fluffy mashed potatoes, or a fine bread and butter pudding made with plumped sultanas. Swoon food. Nostalgic food. Slow food. Food that belongs with big Beethoven symphonies – unlike fast food, which goes better with Kenny Gee and his irritating saxophone.

Comfort food revives, fortifies, encourages, and cheers.

A good meal soothes the soul as it regenerates the body. From the abundance of it flows a benign benevolence. A good and copious dinner begets a mellowing influence; it permeates the bosom with a bland philanthropy of sentiment, embracive of all classes, sects and races of man.
FREDERICK W. HACKWOOD *Good Cheer* 1911

Endeavour Chowder

One of the great feats of our time has been the construction of the full sized replica of James Cook's 'Endeavour'. I was shown around the ship by Project Manager John Longley, who told me something of the foods served to the original sailors. One of the most common dishes was a fish soup chowder, a pale shadow of this adaptation made to suit today's palates.

Serves 4

INGREDIENTS

1 cup of water

1 litre low salt fish stock (or chicken)

2 glasses of white wine

2 carrots, chopped

2 sticks celery, chopped

1 large onion studded with 10 cloves

sprig thyme, parsley and bay leaf tied together

2 kg mixed fish (1 large or several small ones, cleaned and scaled)

few strands saffron (optional)

1 tbsp cornflour

1 can corn (no added salt), drained

1 bunch parsley, chopped

pepper to taste

METHOD

Into large pan put water, stock, white wine, carrots, celery, onion and herbs. Simmer for 1 hour.

Add fish and simmer slowly until fish is cooked – about 20 minutes, depending on size of fish. Large fish may take longer. Remove fish, strain liquor and return it to pan.

Add saffron and boil to reduce it to two-thirds of its volume.

Remove fish from the bones and break into bite-sized pieces and set aside some carrot and celery pieces.

In a small bowl stir a couple of tablespoons of water into the cornflour. Slowly add some stock liquor, a tablespoon at a time, stirring constantly. When the mixture has a creamy consistency pour it into the large pan and stir well into the stock liquor.

Reduce heat, add corn, carrot, celery, parsley and fish. Serve with large spoonsful of fishy bits.

Lentil Soup with Mint and Paprika

The Turkish people have a very healthy cuisine which makes much use of breads and pulses, chick peas, beans and lentils. One of the most pleasant discoveries on a recent trip to Istanbul was Ezo Gelin Corbasi, a lentil soup served with paprika and mint.

Serves 6

INGREDIENTS

200g red lentils, soaked in water overnight, rinsed and drained

1.5 litres good chicken stock or consomme

2 medium onions, finely chopped or grated

2 tbsp tomato paste

2 tbsp extra virgin olive oil

1 tsp paprika

1 cup finely chopped fresh mint

METHOD

Put all ingredients except paprika and mint into large stock pot or heavy saucepan.

Simmer for one-and-a-half hours. Stir in paprika and mint and simmer a further five minutes.

Pork Hock and Lentil Soup

The lentil is one of nature's smallest vitamin pills. It contains B-group vitamins, thiamin, niacin and B6. It's also supercharged with minerals, potassium, magnesium and zinc. Here, it is teamed with bacon hocks – or shanks – to make a robust and nourishing soup. If the bacon has been salt cured and/or smoked, soak it in water overnight before using.

Serves 6

INGREDIENTS

2 medium carrots, finely diced
1 leek, washed and finely cut
1 celeriac, peeled and diced or
   1 cup chopped celery
4 or 5 cloves garlic, crushed
2$\frac{1}{2}$ tbsp oil (preferably a
   strongly flavoured olive oil)
200g red lentils, well washed
   and drained
$\frac{1}{2}$ tsp grated nutmeg
$\frac{1}{2}$ tsp ground fennel seed
6 tbsp finely chopped parsley
3 tbsp finely chopped mint
1 bacon hock, all fat removed
1 litre chicken, veal or
   vegetable stock
60g grated parmesan cheese
pepper to taste

METHOD

In a stock pot or large saucepan gently cook the carrots, leek, celeriac or celery and garlic in 1 tablespoon oil for 3-4 minutes.

Add drained lentils and stir while continuing to cook for about 30 seconds. Stir in nutmeg and fennel.

Stir in about 2 tablespoons of the parsley and 1 tablespoon of the mint. Reserve the remainder for the pesto sauce.

Add the bacon hock and stock, put on the lid and simmer soup very slowly for at least one-and-a-half hours.

Meanwhile, make up a pesto sauce by pounding in a mortar (or blending) the remaining parsley and mint with the parmesan cheese and 1$\frac{1}{2}$ tablespoons oil until a smooth paste is achieved. Season with pepper.

When hock is cooked, remove and cut meat into bite-sized pieces.

To serve: Put bacon pieces into individual soup bowls, pour over soup and top with a spoonful of the pesto sauce.

Serving suggestion: Accompany with crusty bread.

Leftover potential: Keeps well for several days in the refrigerator.

Pork Hock and Lentil Soup

Parmenter's Potato Potage

Parmenter's Potato Potage

An Australian variation of a French soup classic, Potage Parmentier, named after the man who introduced potatoes to the French people.

Serves 8

INGREDIENTS

1 kg potatoes, peeled and cut into 3 or 4 cm cubes

1.5 litres chicken, veal or light vegetable stock

3 or 4 slender young leeks, cut into 5mm thick slices

2 tbsp extra virgin olive oil

1 x 10cm strip orange rind

½ tsp turmeric

1 tsp fennel seed

2 or 3 rashers lean bacon, cut into strips

1 egg yolk

½ tsp grated nutmeg (or mace)

1 tbsp chopped parsley

4 slices white bread, crusts removed, brushed with olive oil, diced and browned in a dry pan on stove or in oven

1 tbsp chopped chives (optional)

METHOD

Put potatoes and stock into a stock pot or large saucepan and simmer for 30 minutes until potatoes are cooked.

Meanwhile, sauté leeks in oil for 10 minutes. Add orange rind, turmeric and fennel seed and cook for 1 minute longer. Add bacon and cook for 5 minutes.

When potatoes are cooked, drain and pour stock over leek mixture. Place half the potatoes into a bowl. Add egg yolk, nutmeg and parsley and mash. Put mashed potato into a piping bag fitted with a large nozzle.

Crush the remaining potato through a sieve and stir into the stock mixture.

To serve: Pipe islands of mashed potato into the centre of individual warmed soup bowls and pour soup around it. Sprinkle with croutons and chives (if using).

Leftover potential: The soup keeps for 2 or 3 days in the refrigerator.

Hint: You could avoid the piping exercise and just spoon the mashed potato into the middle of the bowls.

Minestrone

Beans, pasta, fresh vegetables, cheese and herbs combine to make a glorious main meal soup.

Serves 8

INGREDIENTS

1 onion, roughly chopped

1 stick celery, roughly chopped

2 medium carrots, roughly chopped

2 tbsp extra virgin olive oil

1 litre chicken or vegetable stock

1 leek, cut into thin rings discarding dense green parts

1 dozen stringless beans, cut into 4cm pieces

1 x 425g can tomatoes

1 tsp each of chopped fresh basil, oregano and parsley (if available)

1 tsp minced garlic

2 tbsp hard Italian style cheese (pecorino, romano or parmesan)

1 cup cooked macaroni

1 x 425g can beans (kidney or haricot), drained

1 x 425g can chick peas, drained

METHOD

In a large pan, simmer onion, celery and carrots in 1 tablespoon of the oil for five or six minutes.

Pour in chicken stock and add leek, stringless bean pieces and tomatoes.

Add water to cover and simmer vegetables slowly for at least an hour.

Make up a pesto-type paste by mixing together the other 1 tablespoon oil, the chopped herbs, garlic and the cheese.

Once the soup is cooked add macaroni, canned beans and canned chick peas.

Stir in pesto-type paste and serve sprinkled with cheese.

Tasmanian Onion Soup

So called because the best version I ever made was with Tasmanian onions, grown slowly in the volcanic soils in the north of the island. Based on the traditional French onion soup, this delight makes the perfect winter lunch.

Serves 6

INGREDIENTS

1 kg onions, thinly sliced

50g butter

1 tsp sugar

200ml red wine

1 litre low salt stock (veal,
    chicken or vegetable)

pepper

french bread

soft ripened cheese (brie or
    camembert)

METHOD

Gently cook onions with butter and sugar for a few minutes until onions start to brown. Stir in wine. Cook for a further 10 minutes. Add stock and pepper and simmer gently for 45 minutes.

Before serving cut slices of french bread, spread with butter and put in hot oven for two or three minutes to brown.

To serve, put a couple of pieces of french bread into each individual serving bowl, pour over soup, top with soft-ripened cheese.

Put individual bowls under grill to brown.

Paris Postcard

I found the tomb of A. A. Parmentier particularly interesting. The simple grave site in Paris was planted not with flowers, but with potatoes.

Weather fine. Food fantastic. Prices likewise. April in Paris, anytime in Paris, wish I were here... more often. I love Paris whatever the season, and while the city may no longer be the world's gastronomic capital, it does provide some of the finest food experiences, and some lessons for passionate consumers. It did for me.

Lesson 1: The arrival

The best way to arrive in Paris is by rail. Arrival by air gets you started on the back foot. By the time you've breathed a few lungs full of Charles de Gaulle's air – from the airport of that name – and found a cab, and crawled round the ring road to the centre of Paris – with the driver protesting he doesn't understand where you want to get to – and you feel that where you want to get to is straight back on the plane. But by rail, especially if coming from London on the three-hour Eurostar, you arrive right at the heart of things, fresh and invigorated. And if you opt for a first-class ticket, very well fed and watered. First-class meals with wine are included in the price. And no-one expects a tip. However, it is the last time that happens. Now, you're in France.

Lesson 2: Get a porter

And before you can say "Fifty francs, oui monsieur" he will have whisked your luggage – and anything else on the platform – past the cab queues and into a waiting taxi. I know that 50 francs is a lot ($12.50), but he'll make sure your taxi knows where it is going.

Lesson 3: Studio apartments

These are available for stays of more than a few days. They can seem little bigger than a Paris hotel broom cupboard, but the advantages are several. First, you won't find yourself checked in on the sixth floor of a building without a lift but with a timber stairwell that is a death trap. Second, because these studio apartments are modern you won't find them plastered with large flower-patterned wallpaper. Third, because they have kitchen facilities you can self-cater, buying local produce and eating it chez vous when you want to avoid paying restaurant prices. This is especially valuable at breakfast time where locally bought fresh strawberries, a baguette, Normandie butter, apricot conserve, take-away café crème, and a bottle of Veuve Cliquot brought in should cost less than breakfast for two in an hotel.

Lesson 4: Eating out

The 'busy restaurant theory' is blown out of the H2Eau.

   You probably know the old adage that a busy restaurant must be a good restaurant. Wrong. Looking for a cheap and cheerful bistro in Montparnasse, my love and I walked down a street that appeared to specialise in creperies (pancake restaurants, cheap eats). If it had been Shrove Tuesday I suppose it might have been busier, but on this Monday night King Kong could have lumbered around without attracting attention. There was not a soul in sight, except at one creperie. It was packed with noisy patrons. There was one small table made just for us. Or so we thought.

The manager, a mountain of a man wearing a brown shirt, thigh-hugging black trousers, and black riding boots, gave us the kind of welcome you would expect if you had just walked in from a Paris sewers tour. We were grumpily shown to the table and given a menu. The first thing we noticed was that the only sign of crepe at this establishment would have been the soles of diners' shoes. There were no pancakes in evidence either on the menu or on any of our neighbours' plates.

The other things I couldn't help noticing were the black tablecloths and the wall decorations made up of front pages from war time editions of French newspapers. These depicted such historical moments as the arrival in Paris of Hitler's troops.

The patrons – all in their 50s, 60s and 70s – were drinking large jugs of beer and singing German marching songs. We were suddenly aware that we were in a neo-nazi hang out.

What to do? We did not want to leave and risk causing offence. So we ordered a wiener schnitzel with sauerkraut and some Alsatian wine, said "Ya, danke" a lot, and got out as quickly as we could.

Lesson 5: Vive le shopping

The Paris department stores are fabulous, but avoid eating in them. Take Galleries Lafayette. Large and welcoming – like David Jones with attitude.

Try walking around one of these palaces of consumerism for an hour or so and your blood

High Lunch at Galleries Lafayette

sugar levels will have slumped into oblivion and you'll be looking for sustenance. There is a refreshment hall, but the only impressive thing here are its prices. But life is meant to be experienced, so we tried a light lunch. For two sandwiches – reminiscent of British Rail at its worst – a plastic cup of Beaujolais so new the juice had hardly fermented, and a similar plastic cup of warm milk with a tea bag in it:

$29. And that was for self-service. Plus, we had to eat it perched on top of those high stools, which leave you feeling more like a budgie than a diner.

Lesson 6: Eat a good lunch

After the high lunch experience, we dashed across the Seine to the Left Bank, where little cafés abound. In such places you never know

who you will meet. Such as Vidal Sassoon. He and I have very little in common. He is used to hair, and lots of it. I am not. But what we did have in common was that we were both in the same eatery and I had just written an article about driving around rural France. In it I had said the roads had more hairpins than Vidal Sassoon. I felt I should tell him about the coincidence, and as soon as we had finished some sausage preserved in oil, a warm salad of chicken livers with endive, a large amount of French bread, and a pichet (small jug) of wine – all for $40 – I did. Surrounded by bright young things, Vidal was extremely gracious and asked us back to the Ritz to help him celebrate something important (his 30th or 40th year of dressing hair in Paris, I think) but I had to decline. We had other plans (see Lesson 7).

Lesson 7: Tomb it may concern

Père Lachaise cemetery is a must for the visitor to Paris. This exciting place – unusual for a cemetery and great for a post-lunch stroll – is where anyone who was anyone is buried. An inexpensive map shows you where Edith Piaf, Oscar Wilde, Victor Hugo, Chopin, and the noted gastronomes Brillat-Savarin, Escoffier and A. A. Parmentier are laid to rest. Not that they get much rest with the tourists clomping around overhead. Hectare upon hectare of stone and marble edifices commemorating the great are studied by the curious living.

I found the grand chef Escoffier's tomb was something of a non-event, whereas that of A. A. Parmentier – the man who popularised potatoes with the French – was impressive. Of course I was particularly interested in his edifice, because of a possible family connection. Parmentier's simple grave site was planted not with flowers, but with potatoes, and three or four new potatoes held pride of

place on his stone. A far cry from the grave of Jim Morrison. Here was indeed a sight. A large, noisy group of fans of the late Doors band member were holding a vigil at the late guitarist's plot, drinking beer and wine, smoking non-tobacco substances, playing out of tune guitars, and daubing graffiti over neighbouring tombs, in which the occupants must have been turning. I understand Morrison's remains have now been removed to his place of origin, leaving his former co-residents finally to rest in peace.

Père Lachaise is one of Paris's most fascinating attractions.

Lesson 8: Parlez-vous

Contrary to popular mythology, the Parisians are not hostile to people who do not speak their language. They also appreciate anyone who makes a stab at a bit of French. The following should suffice for most occasions (written semi-phonetically for convenience): "Bonzhoor Mussewer/dam, jer sweez Oztraylay-anne ay zhaddor La Frahnce ay lay shows Frahnsayz. Zhe regrett ker say tooss ker zhe say dear ahn Frahnsay!" meaning, good day Mr and Mrs, I am Australian and I adore France and things French. I regret that that is all I can say in French. A little sycophantic, but after that you should be able to get by.

Also worth remembering. If someone offers you something and you would like it, don't say "merci". It's a way of saying thanks, but no thanks. "Oui, s'il vous plait" would be better.

Lesson 9: A final tip

Waiters make their livings from gratuities, so if you find yourself followed out of the restaurant by an irate garçon, it's probably not because he fancies you. The chances are you haven't done the right thing.

Bonne Chance, Bon Appétit and Bon Voyage!

Oriental Duck Soup

Even quite a big duck feeds only a small number of people. There are, however, plenty of leftover bits to make stock and soup.

Serves 4

INGREDIENTS

Basic stock

1 duck carcass and leftover meat (approximately 1 kg total)

1 x 375g can chicken consomme

2 tbsp tamari soya sauce

2 tbsp mirin

1 tbsp dark soya sauce

3 cloves garlic, crushed

1 medium onion, roughly chopped

1 stick cinnamon

1 whole star anise

1 tsp szechuan pepper

Duck soup

3 or 4 spring onions, finely sliced

1 cup bean sprouts

2 cups cooked noodles (such as hokkien)

100g button mushrooms, cooked

1 x 5cm piece peeled ginger, cut lengthways into very thin strips

1 tbsp Thai-style sweet chilli sauce

METHOD

To make the stock: Chop duck carcass into five or six pieces. Put duck and other stock ingredients into a stock pot or large saucepan. Add water to cover. Bring to the boil and simmer gently for about 45 minutes.

Strain, return stock to a clean pot and reduce over medium heat for 15 minutes. Remove any meat from the carcass, shred and reserve.

Cool reduced stock and refrigerate overnight. When stock is cold, skim fat from the surface. The stock is ready for use.

For the soup: Put stock into a stock pot or large saucepan and bring to the boil. Reduce heat, add spring onions, bean sprouts, noodles, mushrooms, ginger, chilli sauce and reserved duck meat. Warm through and season to taste.

Leftover potential: Keeps for a day or so in the refrigerator.

Burgundian Cheese Balls

A popular appetiser in the Burgundy district of France, Gougères Bourguignonnes are small choux pastry balls baked with cheese and served warm. Delicious and easy to make.

Serves 10 as an appetiser

INGREDIENTS

125g unsalted butter, chopped
250ml water
1 tsp salt
125g plain flour
4 eggs
2 tbsp grated parmesan cheese
100g gruyère cheese, cut into 2cm cubes

METHOD

Put butter, water and salt into a saucepan. Bring to boil and boil for 1 minute. With pan still on heat, add flour all at once, stirring constantly. When mixture comes away from sides of pan as a glossy mass, remove from heat and cool slightly.

Beat in eggs, one at a time, and beat well to combine. Stir in 1 tablespoon parmesan cheese.

Onto a non-stick baking tray, put generous heaped teaspoons of mixture (or you could use a piping bag). Press a cube of gruyère cheese into each mound of mixture and sprinkle with remaining parmesan cheese. Bake at 190°C for 15-20 minutes or until puffed and brown.

Leftover potential: Best eaten straight out of the oven.

Kidney and Bacon Croustade

I grew up loving offal, especially kidneys. In this recipe they are combined beautifully with the smokiness of bacon in a rich red wine sauce served in a bread case.

Serves 6

INGREDIENTS

1 loaf of white bread, unsliced
1 whole veal kidney, trimmed
    and diced and soaked in
    milk for one hour
1 tbsp oil
1 large onion, diced
200g bacon, diced
100ml red wine
200ml veal or beef stock
24 baby spinach leaves

METHOD

To make the croustade, cut all the crust off the bread. Cut into six large cubes.

Lightly toast in a hot oven, then hollow out the centres to create open-ended boxes. The sides should be about 1cm thick.

Drain the kidney pieces and pat dry.

Put the oil in a hot pan, sear the kidney pieces, then add onion and bacon and sauté for approximately 2 minutes.

Deglaze the pan with the wine and stock, bring to the boil. Season to taste.

Serving suggestion: Arrange the spinach leaves on individual plates, put the bread box in the middle, spoon kidneys into the centre and spoon over the sauce.

Wine choice: Nothing beats a Brown Brothers 1994 Cabernet Sauvignon with this kidney dish.

Tofu and Pawpaw Soup

A wonderfully fragrant soup which is good served hot or cold.

Serves 4

INGREDIENTS

400g to 500g fresh ripe
   pawpaw, peeled
2 tbsp chopped white part
   only of spring onions
2 tsp minced garlic
2 tsp minced ginger
2 tsp peanut or olive oil
1 tsp sesame oil
2 tsp minced chilli (or chilli
   sauce)
1 piece lemon grass, crushed
   (optional)
2 kaffir lime leaves, finely
   sliced (optional, or you could
   use a strip of lemon rind)
juice of 2 limes (or 1 tbsp
   lemon juice)
2 tsp ground coriander
750ml chicken or vegetable
   stock
150g tofu (more if you love it)
2 tbsp coconut milk

To serve

thin strips of red capsicum
2 tbsp chopped roasted
   peanuts
2 tbsp finely chopped
   coriander leaves
green part only of spring
   onions, finely chopped

METHOD

Remove seeds from pawpaw and dice flesh.

In a stock pot or large saucepan, sauté spring onions, garlic and ginger in the oils until soft. Add chilli and cook for 30 seconds longer. Add lemon grass and lime leaves (if using), lime juice and ground coriander, then stir in stock and pawpaw and simmer for 15 minutes.

Strain mixture into a clean saucepan. Add tofu and heat for 5 minutes or until warmed through.

Just before serving, remove from heat and stir in coconut milk.

Serving suggestion: Ladle soup into warm bowls and garnish with capsicum, peanuts, coriander leaves and spring onions.

Leftover potential: Keeps for 24 hours in the refrigerator.

Pork and Prawn Wontons and Red Dipping Sauce

These snacks are very simple to prepare. They may be either deep-fried, or poached in a homemade chicken stock and served using the stock as a soup.

Makes 36

INGREDIENTS

wonton wrappers
oil for deep frying or chicken
    stock for simmering

Filling

250g minced pork
250g minced prawn meat
2 tbsp finely chopped
    coriander leaves
2 cloves garlic, finely chopped
1 tsp finely chopped or minced
    ginger
1 tsp chilli sauce
1 tbsp fish sauce
1 tsp caster sugar
$1/2$ tsp five spice powder

Dipping sauce

2 tsp hot chilli sauce
2 tsp tamari soya sauce
2 tbsp mirin
2 cloves garlic, minced or
    finely chopped
1 tbsp finely chopped
    coriander leaves
1 tbsp rice wine vinegar
1 tbsp palm or caster sugar

METHOD

To make the filling: Mix together filling ingredients. Put 1 teaspoon of filling in the centre of each wonton wrapper, then draw the corners together and twist to form small bundles.

Heat oil in a large saucepan and deep-fry wontons until crispy, or poach in simmering stock for 5 minutes.

To make the red dipping sauce: Mix together all ingredients to dissolve sugar.

Leftover potential: The wontons should be eaten immediately. The sauce keeps well in an airtight container in the refrigerator for several days.

Hint: A homemade stock is perfect for poaching the wontons.

Hot Tamales with Chilli Tomato Salsa

This is a Mexican classic. Small savoury parcels are steamed and served hot with a cool salsa of fresh tomatoes, herbs, lemon and olive oil. They should be served chilli hot, but are also tasty served mild. The amounts of chilli I have included make medium-hot tamales.

Makes 20

INGREDIENTS

1 sweet corn cob

2 cups masa harina flour

1 cup good oil (such as olive, walnut or macadamia)

500ml chicken stock

100g chopped cooked chicken

50g chopped black olives

½ medium onion, finely chopped

2 tsp minced chilli

Salsa

500g peeled, seeded and finely diced tomatoes

2 cloves garlic, finely chopped

1 tbsp chopped oregano leaves (or 1 tsp dried oregano)

1 tbsp chopped basil leaves

2 tbsp lemon juice

2 tsp minced chilli

2 tbsp olive oil

pepper to taste

METHOD

Cut 20 squares of non-stick baking paper each measuring approximately 15cm.

Cut corn kernels away from the cob. Break into individual kernels and brown in a dry saucepan over medium heat for about 5 minutes.

Mix together masa harina flour and oil. Add chicken stock, a little at a time. Mix constantly, until a smooth, but firm, dough is formed.

Mix together corn, chicken, olives, onion and chilli and gently fold into the dough.

Roll about a dessertspoon of dough into a small sausage shape and place on a square of the baking paper. Wrap up to make a parcel. Repeat to use all papers and/or dough.

Place parcels in a bamboo, or other, steamer and steam for 30 minutes.

To make salsa: Mix together all salsa ingredients.

Leftover potential: Best eaten the day they're made.

Twice-cooked Kervella Goat Cheese Soufflés

I acquired this recipe from Gary Jones, an exceptionally talented chef whose Perth restaurant, San Lorenzo, won the prestigious Remy Gourmet Restaurant of the Year Award in the mid-1990s. This dish makes a great entree which, because, of its richness, should be followed by a light main course. Gary uses Gabrielle Kervella's goat cheese from WA, but you could substitute with other goat cheese.

Serves 10

INGREDIENTS

½ cup freshly grated
    parmesan cheese plus
    2 tbsp extra
1 litre full-cream milk
1 medium onion
1 bay leaf
3 cloves
200g unsalted butter
200g plain flour
240g goat cheese, roughly
    chopped
10 egg yolks
½ tsp ground nutmeg
½ tsp cayenne pepper
salt and pepper to taste
12 egg whites
500ml whipping cream

METHOD

Grease ten 1-cup capacity ramekins or cups with butter. Sprinkle with some of the parmesan cheese to coat.

Heat the milk in a large saucepan until almost boiling. Remove from heat, add onion, bay leaf and cloves and stand to infuse for 10 minutes.

Melt butter in a separate saucepan, stir in flour and cook over medium heat for 1 minute.

Strain milk and slowly pour into the butter/flour mixture. Cook, stirring frequently, until a thick sauce forms. Add the goat cheese and ¼ cup of parmesan cheese.

When cheese has melted, whisk in egg yolks and beat well. Add nutmeg, cayenne pepper and a pinch of salt and pepper. Whisk egg whites until stiff peaks form, then fold into cheese mixture.

Divide mixture between prepared ramekins. Place on baking trays and bake at 170°C for 20 minutes. Remove from oven and set aside for 30 minutes.

Turn soufflés out into ovenproof dishes, sprinkle with remaining parmesan cheese and pour over cream.

Bake at 180°C for 10 minutes, then brown under a preheated grill until golden.

Leftover potential: Poor.

Nutty Kangaroo Rolls with Chilli Port Sauce

Kangaroo is combined with macadamia nuts, onion, mint, basil and other tasty ingredients, then wrapped in filo pastry and baked. Serve with a Chilli Port Sauce.

Serves 4

METHOD

Mix together kangaroo, egg, mustard, breadcrumbs, nuts and mint. Divide mixture into eight portions and roll into sausage shapes. Set aside in a cool place.

In a frying pan, sweat onion, capsicum and mushrooms in 1 tablespoon olive oil over low heat until soft. Remove pan from heat and stir in basil and peanut butter.

On to a damp, but not wet, tea towel, place two sheets of filo pastry. Brush top sheet with a little oil, turn over both sheets together and brush again.

Cover filo pastry with a few spinach leaves, leaving a space at each end so you can fold the pastry to make a parcel. Cover with a little of the onion mixture, top with a kangaroo sausage and a little more onion mixture, then cover with a few more spinach leaves.

Fold ends of pastry over other ingredients and roll up to make a parcel. Repeat with remaining ingredients to make eight parcels.

Brush rolls with oil, place on an oiled baking tray and bake at 190°C for 20 minutes or until golden.

To make the sauce: Combine all ingredients in a saucepan and cook over medium heat until the mixture reduces by half and thickens.

Leftover potential: Keeps well for two or three days in the refrigerator. May be eaten hot or cold.

INGREDIENTS

500g minced kangaroo
1 egg
1 tbsp dijon-style mustard
2 tbsp breadcrumbs
    (preferably made from day
    old bread)
50g macadamia (or other
    nuts), chopped
1 tbsp finely chopped mint
1 small onion, finely chopped
2 tbsp finely chopped red or
    yellow capsicum
2 tbsp finely chopped button
    mushrooms
1 tbsp olive oil plus extra for
    brushing pastry
1 tbsp chopped fresh basil
1 tbsp crunchy peanut butter
1 bunch spinach leaves,
    washed and drained
16 sheets filo pastry

For chilli port sauce
300ml port wine
250ml veal or chicken stock
1 tbsp white wine vinegar
2 tbsp Thai-style sweet chilli
    sauce

Fondues Bruxelloises (Fried Cheese Balls)

These fondues bear no relation to what we normally think of as fondues. Rather, they are deep-fried cheese squares, which could have been the inspiration behind deep-frying camembert cheese. This is a much more cost-effective way of deep-frying cheese and is a very popular Belgian entree.

Serves 12 as an appetiser

INGREDIENTS

100g butter
150g plain flour
500ml milk
150g swiss cheese (emmental
    or gruyère), grated
100g parmesan cheese, grated
¼ tsp cayenne pepper
½ tsp grated nutmeg
6 egg yolks
salt and white pepper to taste
3 eggs
2 tsp water
1 tbsp oil
flour for dusting
breadcrumbs
oil for deep frying

METHOD

The day before, or the morning of the day of serving …
melt butter in heavy based saucepan. Stir in flour. When mixed, gradually stir in milk. Bring to boiling point and cook, stirring constantly, over low heat for 2 minutes. Remove pan from heat, stir in cheeses and mix until melted.

Return to heat, add cayenne pepper, nutmeg, the 6 egg yolks and salt and pepper. Simmer, stirring constantly, for 3 minutes. Do not allow the mixture to boil.

Pour mixture into a greased or oiled 23 x 32cm baking tin lined with baking paper. Spread mixture evenly over base of tin, then cover with a sheet of baking paper and set aside to cool. When cool, put in the refrigerator. You could speed the process by putting the mixture in the freezer – but don't allow it to freeze solid.

The next day (or later in the day) …
beat the 3 eggs until frothy, mix in water, oil and a little salt and pepper.

Turn cheese mixture out and roll into sausage shapes or balls about the size of large fish fingers. Dust each sausage with flour, then dip into egg mixture and shake off excess. Roll in breadcrumbs and again shake off excess.

Deep-fry until golden and drain on paper towels.

Serving suggestion: Serve on shredded lettuce leaves.

Leftover potential: Poor.

Hint: Once egged and breadcrumbed, the fondues will keep well in the freezer. I like to serve half as an appetiser for a dinner of six and reserve the rest for another occasion.

Fondues Bruxelloises

Samosas

Samosas

One of my favourite snack foods, Indian savoury parcels are a great way of using up leftovers, such as peas and mashed potato. They may be made vegetarian or with meat.

Serves 4

INGREDIENTS

1 tsp minced ginger
1 tsp minced garlic
1 tbsp finely chopped onion
1 tbsp olive or peanut oil
1 tsp curry powder
1 tsp ground coriander
125g minced meat (or
    chopped mushroom,
    prawns or fish)
1 tsp garam masala
1 tsp cornflour
1 tbsp stock
2 tbsp finely chopped
    coriander leaves (or
    parsley, mint or a
    combination of the two)
50g mashed potatoes
50g cooked peas
spring roll wrappers
oil for deep frying

Dip

3 tbsp finely chopped mint
3 tbsp salt reduced soya
    sauce
3 tsp sesame oil
½ tsp white pepper

METHOD

Gently fry ginger, garlic and onion in oil until onion softens. Stir in curry powder and ground coriander and continue cooking for 2-3 minutes.

Add meat (or substitute) and cook for 2 minutes. Stir in garam masala.

Mix cornflour with stock, stir into mixture and cook to thicken it.

Stir in fresh coriander (or other herbs), mashed potatoes and peas to make up the filling.

Cut spring roll wrappers into strips about 8cm wide. Put a small dollop of filling mixture on leading edge and fold up.

When all parcels are made, heat oil in a large saucepan and deep-fry samosas until golden and heated through.

Meanwhile, make up dipping sauce by mixing together all ingredients.

Leftover potential: Once cooked the samosas should be eaten immediately, but they may be frozen once assembled and cooked from frozen – remember to allow a little extra cooking time.

Stir Crazy

If there's one fast food that is worth considering, it's the stir-fry. It involves so many senses – sight, smell, sound, touch – and is one of the simplest.

One of the most impressive sights I have seen was at Singapore's Seafood Centre on the east coast. It is here that four seafood restaurants cater for some 6,000 patrons a night. Dining at the Red House restaurant, I was invited to watch a near miracle: a dish of stir-fried chilli crab cooked in less than one minute! The chef – one of 50 or so working at a long line of wok burners – had had all the food prepared for him. His job was to cook it.

Taking his well-seasoned wok, he launched it on to a burner, planted his foot on a gas pedal and a massive burner roared into life. Using only his ladle, he splashed oil into the hot wok, followed it with an assortment of spices, ginger, garlic and chilli, some sugar and a white powder which could have been salt, or MSG, and a red syrup which looked just like tomato ketchup – and may well have been.

In went fresh crabs, cut in two, cleaned, and with claws cracked for ease of eating. After tossing the mixture for a few moments – and adding a little stock to keep the mixture moist – it was cooked. The foot off the pedal, the gas died down, the chef swung round, tossed the delightfully aromatic concoction on to a plate and it was whisked to the table, with this passionate consumer in hot pursuit. It was – I hardly need say – bliss! The chef, meanwhile, was halfway through cooking his next dish, and by the time I left the restaurant would have cooked a hundred more.

If there's one fast food that is worth considering, it's the stir-fry. This form of cooking, which involves so many senses – sight, smell, sound, touch – is one of the simplest. It's also a way of keeping fats to a minimum and locking the flavours in vegetables, fish, seafood and meat.

There is no mystery to stir-frying, but many cooks are disappointed when the results are far from what they expected, with meat being tough, seafood overcooked and dry, vegetables mushy, mushrooms soggy. Ingredients stewing instead of frying. A few pointers should help to guarantee success every time.

The heat

This is the most important factor for successful stir-frying. Although some new stoves now boast a wok ring, the heat is still significantly less than you need to do more than a small amount of food at a time. For the technically minded, a standard gas ring delivers around 10 megajoules and a domestic wok ring around 17 megajoules. When you realise a commercial turbo wok burner can deliver a massive 140 megajoules you can imagine how difficult it can be to cook as well as a chef in a restaurant kitchen. In addition, with a commercial unit, the wok sits in the heat, whereas with a domestic version it sits over the heat, allowing heat to 'spill'.

The wok

Several materials are used to make woks. My preference is for iron woks, made either of cast iron or mild steel. Cast iron woks are heavier and slower to heat up, but the surface can be seasoned, making it virtually non-stick. This can be done by repeatedly heating the wok and coating it with a film of oil. A cast iron wok should not be washed with strong detergent, since it will remove the oil treatment.

Mild steel woks are the most commonly used, and are cheap – at around $10 from most Asian food stores. These utensils come with a protective coating and this has to be removed before use. The best way to do this is to fill with a strong bicarbonate of soda mixture (4 tablespoons to a litre of water) and to allow to simmer for a half hour. Scrub with a scourer and repeat the process as required to completely remove any traces of coating. The wok should then be seasoned by smearing with oil and heating several times, rinsing with hot water between each treatment. Leave a light surface of oil on the wok.

Once seasoned, I avoid using scourers or strong detergent on the wok.

Mild steel woks heat very quickly and should not be allowed to burn. Once cooking is completed, they should be washed immediately, dried and then heated quickly and wiped with a light coating of oil before putting away.

On the down side, mild steel can rust. This means that acidic sauces – such as using lemon juice – may strip the oiled coating. Foods should not be left in these woks. And care should be taken not to scratch with metal

implements or the wok will need re-seasoning. I'm told Singaporean cooks often season their woks by rubbing with half an onion then frying the onion in peanut oil for a few minutes before rinsing, drying and putting away. It is not a technique I have used.

I don't use stainless steel woks because I find the heat is not even, and food tends to stick. Non-stick cookware manufacturers generally advise not to use high heat with their products. And with stir-frying you have to. There are several good non-stick woks, but they're pricey.

Techniques

There are only a few rules for stir-frying, the main one being to heat the wok before putting in oil and then make sure the oil is hot before ingredients are added.

Use an oil with a high smoke point. I prefer to use peanut or canola oil, seldom olive oil.

Add ingredients in small quantities. If cooking one dish for four people, it is a good idea to cook some of the foods separately and then toss them all through at the last minute to warm. Start with the foods that need the most cooking. If ingredients start to stick, sprinkle in a little water or stock rather than adding more oil.

"Everything you see,
I owe to spaghetti"

SOPHIA LOREN

Pasta, Rice & Noodles

Cold Mixed Noodles Szechuan-Style

Servings 4 to 6

INGREDIENTS
1 pack (350g) fresh chinese
   egg or spinach noodles
2 tsp sesame oil
$1/2$ cucumber, julienned
$1/2$ red bell pepper, julienned
125g fresh mung bean sprouts
2 cups cooked chicken breast,
   shredded

Dressing
$1/3$ cup chicken broth
$1/2$ cup sesame seed paste or
   crunchy peanut butter
2 tbsp soy sauce
2 tbsp rice vinegar
2 tsp sesame oil
2 tsp chilli sauce
$1/2$ tsp sugar
$1/2$ tsp szechuan peppercorns,
   toasted and ground

METHOD
Bring the water to boil in a 9 litre stockpot.

Cook the noodles according to the directions on the package.
Then drain, rinse with cold water, and drain again. Place the
noodles in a bowl, add the sesame oil and toss to coat.

Add the cucumber, bell pepper and mung bean sprouts. Toss
to mix.

To make the dressing: Combine the chicken broth and sesame
seed paste in a bowl. Whisk until blended.

Add all the remaining dressing ingredients and mix well. Pour the
dressing over the noodles and toss before serving.

Serving suggestion: Place the noodles on a service plate
and arrange the chicken over the top. Cover and refrigerate
until chilled.

Malaysian-ish Noodles

A recipe loosely based on the Malaysian dish, Mee Rebus.

Serves 4

INGREDIENTS

600g chicken thigh meat,
   skinned and cut in strips
2 tsp sesame oil
1 tsp szechuan pepper
100g peanuts (or crunchy
   peanut butter)
2 tsp ginger, minced
2 tsp malay curry powder
2 tsp hot chilli sauce
1 tbsp peanut oil
1 spanish onion, finely
   chopped
250ml chicken stock
2 tsp sugar
2 eggs
400g pre cooked hokkien
   noodles
extra peanuts, finely chopped
fresh coriander leaves

METHOD

Marinate the chicken strips in sesame oil and szechuan pepper for at least 20 minutes.

Crush the peanuts with a mortar and pestle (or use a food processor). Pound (or blend) in the ginger, curry powder, and chilli sauce. Cook this paste in the oil with the chopped onion for 3 or 4 minutes.

Add the chicken stock and sugar. Cook for a further 10 minutes to allow the flavours to develop.

Simmer the chicken in this sauce for 25 minutes, very gently.

Make a simple omelette by whisking the eggs with a teaspoon of water. Cook in an oiled pan for a couple of minutes on each side.

Remove to plate or chopping board. Roll up and slice omelette into thin strips.

Blanch the hokkien noodles in boiling water, then drain. Serve the noodles, topped with the chicken in sauce, sliced omelette, extra chopped peanuts, and fresh coriander leaves.

Handy Hint: For added flavour you can make a peanut pesto by grinding two tablespoons of peanuts with several cloves of finely chopped garlic. Then add some chopped coriander leaves and a little peanut oil. Serve on top.

Pasta Hot Stuff

A simple variation of the Roman dish, Buccatini all' Amatriciana, a dish with a chilli hot tomato sauce, which traditionally uses pancetta, salt-cured bacon. I find a good Australian ham makes a suitable substitute. Vegetarians may omit the ham if they wish.

Serves 6

INGREDIENTS

250g pasta pieces
   (buccatini, penne, rigatoni,
   conchiglie, etc)
1 medium onion
1 tbsp extra virgin olive oil
4 or 5 slices reduced salt/fat
   ham (125g)
1 x 425g can tomatoes (no
   added salt)
2 tsp concentrated tomato
   paste
1 tsp sugar
1 tsp chilli sauce or chopped
   fresh chilli
1/2 tsp grated nutmeg

METHOD

Boil pasta in lots of lightly salted water until just cooked. It should still be al dente.

Chop onion finely and cook gently in the olive oil. Once onion is softened, stir in ham, tomatoes, tomato paste, sugar, chilli and nutmeg.

Break up tomatoes and allow the mixture to cook for 15 minutes or so until it has a good, thick consistency. Season to taste. Mix in pasta and allow to warm through.

Serve on its own as an entree or with meat

Turkish Ravioli with Yoghurt and Paprika Dressing

METHOD
To make filling: Mix all ingredients well and set aside.

To make ravioli: On a floured board, make a mound of flour with a well in the centre. Break in eggs and add water. With the fingers (clean) break yolks, work eggs with the water and gradually bring in the flour from the edge of the well. Once all the flour is mixed in, make a ball of the dough and cut in two.

On a floured work surface roll out first ball with a floured rolling pin until the sheet of dough is thin. With a sharp knife, cut into roughly 10cm squares.

Place a teaspoon of beef mixture in the centre of each square. Brush edges with water then pick up edges and squeeze together to form a parcel. Repeat with the rest of the dough.

Once the parcels are made, put a few at a time into rapidly boiling stock to cook. Depending on the size, this will take between five and 10 minutes. Check a parcel after five minutes. Drain and keep warm while you cook the others.

Note: Any leftover dough may be cut into thin strips, left to dry and used like egg noodles.

To make Yoghurt and Paprika Dressing: In a warm bowl, put in yoghurt, garlic, and parsley. Mix well. In a separate pan, heat the olive oil till almost smoking. Sprinkle in paprika. If the oil is hot enough, the paprika will fizz and the oil will change colour. To serve, drain last of ravioli, stir sauce through it. Top with paprika and oil mixture.

Ravioli is not just a dish of Italy – Turkish cooks make it too. In fact, some say they might have invented it! This simple recipe uses freshly made ravioli pasta with a light beef and herb filling, served with a yoghurt and paprika dressing.

Serves 6 as entree, 4 as main course

INGREDIENTS
250g flour, preferably noodle,
  or durum, flour
3 large eggs
1 tbsp water
extra flour for kneading
1 litre veal or chicken stock to
  cook ravioli

Filling
250g finely ground or lean
  minced beef
1 large onion, finely chopped
2 or 3 tbsp finely chopped
  parsley
1/2 tsp pepper

Dressing
300ml natural low fat yoghurt
1 clove garlic, finely chopped
1 tbsp chopped parsley or
  mint (or both)
1 tbsp extra virgin olive oil
1 tsp paprika

Lighter Lasagna

A classic dish with a lighter approach. Use traditional lasagna sheets, cooked until al dente and then drained, or instant pasta sheets.

Serves 8

INGREDIENTS

1 packet traditional lasagna
   sheets, boiled and drained
   (or 1 packet instant lasagna
   sheets)

For the meat sauce

1 tbsp finely chopped onion

2 tbsp extra virgin olive oil

1 carrot, grated

1 stick celery, finely chopped

1 tbsp chopped fresh thyme
   (or 1 tsp dried)

1 kg minced lean beef (or pork
   and veal mixture)

500g tomato pulp

250ml chicken or veal stock

200ml dry white wine

black pepper to taste

For the bechamel sauce

40-50 g unsalted butter

1 heaped tbsp cornflour

1 litre reduced fat milk

250g reduced fat mozzarella
   cheese

100g freshly grated parmesan
   cheese

1/2 tsp grated nutmeg

1 large egg, separated

METHOD

To make the meat sauce: In a frying pan, lightly sauté onion in olive oil for about 2 minutes or until soft. Add carrot and celery and continue cooking gently for 5-6, minutes. Add thyme and meat and cook, stirring constantly, until meat changes colour. Add tomato pulp, stock, wine and pepper. Continue cooking slowly for 20-25 minutes or until mixture becomes a thickish sauce. If using instant lasagna, the sauce should be fairly sloppy. Meanwhile prepare the bechamel sauce.

To make the bechamel sauce: Melt butter in a heavy-based saucepan over medium heat. Stir in cornflour and continue cooking for 2-3 minutes, but make sure you do not allow it to brown.

Slowly stir in milk and simmer, stirring constantly, until sauce starts to thicken. Stir in mozzarella cheese, 1 tablespoon of the parmesan cheese and the nutmeg. When cheeses have melted, check whether any salt is needed and add at this stage. Remove sauce from heat. Stir in egg yolk.

To assemble the lasagna: Use a large baking dish and spread the base with a layer of meat sauce, top with a layer of pasta, then with more meat sauce and some bechamel sauce. Continue layering pasta, meat sauce and bechamel sauce. Finish with a layer of meat sauce and reserve a small amount of bechamel sauce.

Whisk egg white until soft peaks have formed. Fold egg white into reserved bechamel sauce and spread over top of lasagna. Sprinkle with remaining parmesan cheese and bake at 190°C for 45 minutes or until top is brown.

Leftover potential: Good. Keeps well for 2 or 3 days in the refrigerator. I usually make up a fresh cheese sauce topping to pour over before reheating.

Hint: If using instant lasagna sheets, the sauces should be somewhat sloppier than if using fresh lasagna, to allow the sheets to absorb the moisture and to expand.

Crabby Chilli Spaghetti

This simple recipe combines crabs and chilli sauce to make the perfect accompaniment for plain boiled spaghetti. Most crabs are suitable, but try to avoid the Japanese giant spider crab which can measure up to two metres across the claw tips – impossible to get in the pot. To be certain of freshness, buy crabs live.

Serves 6

METHOD

To make the sauce: Pour the oil from the anchovies into a large frying pan, add onion and garlic and cook gently for 3-4 minutes. Stir in tomatoes, chilli sauce, wine, sugar, olives and pepper and simmer until reduced to about one-third of its original volume.

To prepare the crabs: Place live crabs in a bucket of fresh water 2-3 hours to put to sleep painlessly. Pull off the claws and crack with a hammer or mallet. Remove the outer shell from the crabs. Take out the conical-shaped gills from under the shell and wash crabs under cold water to remove all sediment. Break bodies in half lengthwise. Wash again to remove any loose shell. Drain well, but leave wet.

To cook the crabs: Put the bodies and claws in a large saucepan, cover and cook over high heat, shaking pan every few seconds for 2 minutes. The crabs will start to steam in the water they were washed in.

Pour sauce over crabs, reduce heat and cook for 15 minute shaking pan occasionally – do not stir.

Meanwhile, cook spaghetti in lightly salted water with grated nutmeg until al dente. Drain.

Place spaghetti in a large bowl, spoon over crabs and sauce and toss to combine. Serve mountains of this mixture to an appreciative audience, include finger bowls of warm water into which lemon juice has been squeezed.

INGREDIENTS

500g spaghetti
freshly grated nutmeg

Sauce

120g jar anchovies in olive oil
   (Australian of course)
1 large onion, finely chopped
6 cloves garlic, finely chopped
1.5 kg very ripe tomatoes,
   finely chopped
1 tbsp chilli sauce or
   according to taste
375ml white wine
1 tbsp sugar
12 black olives
pepper to taste

The crabs

3 kg green crabs (preferably
   live)

Using your noodle

I lifted the gnocchi dough and deftly waved it to and fro in the manner I had seen done by a Chinese noodle master. At least, that's what I thought.

noodles. They're thin, they're elegant, they're tasty and they're inexpensive. They've also been the cause of my greatest culinary embarassment.

It happened like this. I was visiting my nextdoor neighbour, Mafalda, for a lesson in gnocchi making. A fine cook of Italian descent – with a food garden that is a work of art – Mafalda was preparing a huge batch of the precious pasta for a big family celebration.

As I arrived in her kitchen the scene was one of great concentration and excitement. Surrounded by assorted daughters and daughters-in-law (all the boys were watching the footy) this queen of the culinary arts was kneading the biggest ball of dough I had seen, a joy to behold, pale yellow in colour and beautifully elastic.

I was offered, and accepted a cup of rich, dark espresso coffee, and the first of many cannoli, those wonderful deep-fried canneloni-like pastries filled with pastry cream. The ensemble were busy discussing, in English and Italian, the best way to make gnocchi, the great gnocchi of days gone by, and whether or not they should be made with potato.

While the dough went from family member to family member for kneading, we discussed how Italians from different regions varied the ways they prepared noodles, the use of eggs, whether water needed to be added, or oil.

Eventually, I made a mention of Chinese noodles and asked the gathering whether any of them had witnessed the magic that is the hand-making of Chinese noodles.

"No," they chorused, "how are noodles made in China?"

I explained the process that I had seen – and which I still regard as one of the finest food spectacles. How, starting with a great lump of dough, the noodle maker would stretch it out into a large sausage. Then it would be dusted with flour, folded over, twisted and stretched again by swinging it about a lot. The process would then be repeated, adding more flour each time to prevent the dough from sticking. Fold, flour, twist, stretch.

By now there were puzzled looks on some of the faces around me.

I explained that after repeating this process some seven times there would be 128 strands of noodle, or an extra fold could make 256 strands, but I didn't know what was the norm. I just knew that once you cut the ends off, you were left with beautifully symmetrical strands of noodles. My observations were met with glazed expressions.

I asked for the gnocchi dough, saying that perhaps it would be best if I showed them what I meant. What a mistake that was. I floured my hands then lifted the three kilo mass from the floured workbench, I deftly waved it to and fro in the manner I had seen done by a Chinese noodle master. At least, that's what I thought. Suddenly the dough shook itself free of my grasp and, assisted by gravity, threw itself earthwards.

Its point of impact was an old, well-worn mat. This aged piece of well-loved soft-furnishing was host to a multitude of things, fluff, cat hairs, grains of rice, grit, which soon transferred themselves to the welcoming surface of the dough, which soaked them up like a sponge.

I raised the once pristine mass from the floor with shame in my heart and a pair of size 20 blushes on my cheeks.

"Idiot", "careless fool", "show-off." These are the expressions of abuse I deserved from the spectators of this disaster. Instead, the women were gracious. Some politely stifled laughter, others did not, while Mafalda quickly took a large carving knife from a drawer and deftly hacked off the offending foreign matter and went about the business of shaping the gnocchi. Though invited to, I could not bring myself to stay to sample them.

Moral: Don't play with other people's food. Play with your own.

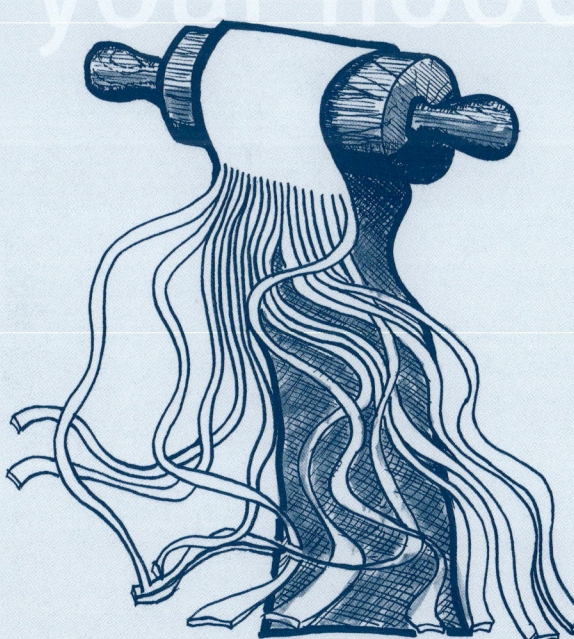

Cooking noodles

○ When cooking noodles, too much water can barely be enough. Allow around 4 litres of water for one 375g packet of dried egg noodles.
○ Dried wheat noodles should be cooked in rapidly boiling water.
○ With rice noodles, cook as close to serving time as possible.
○ If cooking egg noodles in advance, drain and toss in a little oil.
○ Noodles for stewy or soupy dishes may be slightly undercooked, they can continue cooking in the dish in which they are served.
○ Fine noodles, such as rice vermicelli, simply need to sit in very hot water for a few minutes to be ready for use.

Types of noodle

Cellophane noodles: Also known as glass or transparent noodles, these fine noodles are made of mung or broad beans. They come in tied up bundles. Break them up after cooking.

Chinese egg noodles: Made like Italian egg pasta, with flour and eggs. Ideal for stir-fry since they seldom stick together.

Hokkien noodles: Usually sold pre-cooked and coated in oil, these are thick egg noodles somewhat akin in shape to the Italian Spaghetti alla Chitarra. They need rinsing in hot water before use. Ideal for stir-fries.

Japanese noodles: A variety is available, such as Cha Soba, made with buckwheat noodles flavoured with tea; Soba, round stick noodles also made of buckwheat; Ramen noodles, crinkly and usually used in those instant meals where you just pour hot water into a plastic container and finish up with something that tastes just like that; Somen, thin stick noodles made of hard wheat flour and oil; Udon, plump hard wheat noodles; and Kishimen, wider version of Udon noodles.

Pat Thai (Stir-fried Noodles)

This is one of those fabulous dishes I could eat at any time of day or night. It was prepared for me by Tum, one of David Thompson's Thai cooks at the Sailor's Thai Noodle Bar in Sydney's Rocks district. Since the process is very quick, I find it best to cook one portion at a time to guarantee the best results.

Serves 1

INGREDIENTS

1 tsp peanut oil
2 cloves garlic, finely chopped
50g chicken thigh meat, sliced
1 cup rice noodles, soaked in
    water for 2 hours and
    drained
1 tbsp white sugar
2 tbsp thin tamarind water (or
    rice vinegar)
2 tbsp fish sauce
2 tbsp deep-fried hard bean
    curd (available in oriental
    food stores)
1 tbsp dried prawns, soaked
    and dried on paper towel
1 cup bean sprouts
1 tsp shredded salted radish
    (optional)
Stock to moisten mixture
1 egg

METHOD

Heat wok or frying pan over medium heat. When hot add oil and garlic and fry quickly. After a few seconds add chicken and fry until just cooked.

Stir in noodles, sugar, tamarind water and fish sauce. Mix in bean curd, dried prawns, bean sprouts and salted radish (if using). If mixture becomes too dry, add a little stock.

Stir in egg and cook, stirring constantly, until it is just cooked.

To serve: Accompany with peanuts, chilli powder and lime segments.

Leftover potential: This dish is so quick to prepare that it should be cooked and eaten immediately.

Summertime Sauce

A delicious and colourful vegetable sauce seasoned with anchovies, perfect with plain pasta.

Serves 4

INGREDIENTS

2 tbsp olive oil

1 small onion, finely sliced

2 red or yellow capsicums, sliced

2 cloves garlic, finely chopped

1 eggplant, peeled and cubed

1 tbsp finely chopped fresh parsley

12 anchovy fillets, chopped

500g cooked spiral or fusilli pasta

METHOD

Heat oil in a saucepan over medium heat. Add onion and cook, stirring, until golden.

Add capsicums and garlic and cook, stirring frequently, for 10 minutes. Add eggplant and parsley and cook, stirring frequently, for 10 minutes longer. Stir in anchovies and cook for 1-2 minutes longer.

Spoon mixture over hot pasta and serve immediately.

Ricotta and Spinach Cannelloni

Pasta is a fabulous food, high in energy and non-fattening. That is, until you start adding things to it. This recipe uses two light but tasty sauces with cannelloni. The tubular pasta is filled with a ricotta and spinach stuffing, then simmered in tomato sauce before being topped with a light bechamel.

Serves 4

INGREDIENTS

½ medium onion finely
    chopped
3 cloves garlic, peeled and
    crushed
2 tbsp extra virgin olive oil
300ml tomato pulp or puree
    (not the concentrated paste)
½ tsp sugar
1 bunch spinach or 100g
    cooked spinach
250g ricotta cheese
25g parmesan cheese
¼ tsp ground mace or
    nutmeg
white pepper to taste
20g butter
30g cornflour
300ml reduced fat milk
1 cup chopped parsley
12 cannelloni tubes (the kind
    that don't need pre-cooking)

METHOD

Sauté onion and garlic in 1 tablespoon olive oil until softened. Stir in tomato pulp or puree and sugar. Remove from heat. Pour into a baking dish and spread evenly over the base.

Wash spinach and drain. Remove stalks and chop leaves. In the pan in which the sauce was cooked (it is unnecessary to wash the pan), put remaining oil and cook spinach for 2 minutes. Transfer spinach to a mixing bowl and cool slightly. Stir in ricotta cheese, parmesan cheese, mace or nutmeg and white pepper. Allow to cool.

In the same pan (again, washing is unnecessary), melt the butter. Add cornflour and cook, stirring, for 1 minute over low heat. Slowly add milk and cook, stirring constantly, until sauce thickens. Add chopped parsley and season to taste.

With spoon or piping bag, fill the cannelloni tubes with the spinach and cheese mixture. Place the filled tubes on the tomato sauce in the baking dish.

Cover cannelloni with the parsley bechamel sauce and sprinkle with additional parmesan cheese, if you wish.

Cover with foil and bake at 180°C for at least 25 minutes, remove foil and bake for 20 minutes longer to allow the top to brown.

Leftover potential: Good. May be reheated or refreshed by adding more sauce topping.

Ricotta and Spinach Cannelloni

Bean Feast

Bean Feast

Unlike the great Greek geometrical whizz kid Pythagoras, I adore fresh broad beans. He, on the other hand, believed that these innocuous pulses contained the souls of the dead and should, therefore, be avoided. It's the Italians who provide the inspiration for this dish of young, succulent broad beans prepared with pasta. I like to use my own homemade ribbon pasta for this (see recipe for Pasta with Chilli Scallops, page 57) but you could use either fresh purchased pasta or the dried variety.

Serves 4

INGREDIENTS

1 kg fresh broad beans in their
   pods
450g fresh pasta or 375g
   dried egg noodles
4 cloves garlic, finely chopped
2 tbsp extra virgin olive oil
4 tbsp vegetable or chicken
   stock
1 tsp chilli sauce or more
   according to taste
1 tbsp parmesan cheese
   (optional)

METHOD

Remove beans from pods, discarding the very large ones and any that are yellowish.

Cook beans gently in unsalted water until tender. (Salt in the water can make the skins tough.)

Cook the pasta in lightly salted water until al dente. Drain. Meanwhile, in a large frying pan, sauté garlic in oil for 5 minutes or until soft. Add stock and cook until it reduces to about one-third of its original volume. Stir in chilli sauce (it's optional).

Add broad beans and pasta to pan. Toss and serve immediately topped with parmesan cheese (if desired).

Leftover potential: Keeps well for a day or so in the refrigerator, but is best eaten freshly made.

Hint: The beans may be peeled if the skins are tough or the beans are rather large. The cooking time for the broad beans depends on the age of the beans – young fresh beans will only take about 10 minutes, whereas larger more mature beans may take 20 minutes or longer.

Risotto

It's easy to see why this dish is a firm favourite of Italians. They argue that it may only be made with short grain, Arborio rice. Don't you believe it. A delightful risotto may be cooked using Australian medium-grained calrose rice.

Serves 6

INGREDIENTS

1 tbsp olive oil

1 medium onion, finely chopped

2 cups white rice

½ cup white wine (chardonnay)

2 cups chicken stock (low in salt)

½ tsp saffron

25g butter

black pepper

parmesan cheese (optional)

METHOD

Place in pan the olive oil and the chopped onion. Cook gently.

Once softened, about five minutes, add rice and stir well. Allow to cook for about four minutes just to brown the grains of rice, this makes them more nutty. Add wine and chicken stock to cover the rice.

Now add the saffron. Allow to simmer uncovered for 20 minutes, with enough water or stock to at least cover the rice. Make sure the rice doesn't dry out.

At the end of the cooking time the rice will have absorbed most of the stock or water.

Add butter and black pepper and if you prefer some parmesan.

Note: Although the addition of saffron is preferred for its bright yellow colour and its subtle flavour, it is an expensive ingredient. I'd prefer to do without than substitute with other colouring, such as turmeric.

Serving suggestions: This is the basic risotto. It can be served either as an accompaniment to a meat dish or on its own.

As a main meal: Add some vegetables, a few strips of capsicum just lightly stir fried, peas and some chicken that has been poached in chicken stock.

Pasta with Chilli Scallops

Simplicity is the key to much great cooking. It's also the key to the success of the Manfredi family restaurant at the Rocks in Sydney. The mother and son team of Franca and Stefano run belmondo, working in tandem on dishes such as this one. If you choose not to make your own pasta, you will need about 350g of purchased pasta, cook until al dente, then drain.

Serves 4

METHOD

To make the pasta: Put flour in a pile on a well-floured work surface, make a well in the centre, break in the eggs and add the water. Using your fingertips, gradually work the flour into the liquid from the edges, then knead until a firm dough has been achieved, adding more flour if mixture is too sticky.

Feed dough through a pasta machine set to fettuccine thickness. If you don't have a pasta machine, roll dough to required thickness, dust with flour, then roll up and cut into ribbon pasta. Spread out pasta on a floured board.

Mix together garlic, chillies and parsley in a bowl. Add 2 tablespoons olive oil and season with salt and pepper.

Pan-fry scallops in a little oil for a few seconds each side. Take care not to overcook the scallops.

Reduce heat, add half the garlic mixture and warm through. Add pasta to pan, toss and warm through. Add remaining garlic mixture and serve.

Leftover potential: Poor. Best eaten immediately.

INGREDIENTS

4 cloves garlic, finely chopped
2 chillies, seeded and finely chopped
1 tbsp finely chopped Italian parsley
2 tbsp extra virgin olive oil, plus extra for pan-frying
salt and pepper to taste
20 scallops, roes left on

For the pasta

300g plain white flour plus extra for flouring board
3 large eggs (preferably free range)
1 tbsp cold water

Pizza the Action

I decided it was time for action. The boys agreed to light the wood stove, the girls helped me fire up a starter mixture. We were to make pizzas for lunch.

Can there be any sound more irritating than the shriek of a police siren, the scratch of a fingernail on blackboard, or the drone of a budget speech? The answer is: Yes. How about the whine of tetchy teenagers? "I'm bored." "I didn't ask to be born." You know the sort of thing.

While there is no known cure for the disease, there is something which could give temporary palliative help: the pizza. Not so much giving them one, which provides only short term relief, but letting them make pizzas for themselves. This is a technique I have found useful both for distracting offenders for considerable lengths of time as well as for injecting enthusiasm in a worthwhile, hands-on pastime: cooking.

I discovered this for myself when marooned on a farm for a long weekend – a very long weekend – with the offspring of a number of New Age laissez-faire parents, the types of adult whose approach to parenthood is to allow their children to bring themselves up, enabling them to develop their personalities by leaving them to their own devices – these devices being computer games, TVs, videos, and CD players. Remote control child-rearing.

In the rude building in which we were billeted there was no electricity and therefore none of the teenagers' devices would have worked even if they had them with them. On the plus side – for the little darlings, at least – was the fact that there was no hot water,

providing them with an excuse to remain unwashed for the duration.

I suffered the sight of their gloomy countenances, their clothes bedecked with slogans, their shuffling around in undone designer running shoes. But the last straw for this normally tolerant, child-loving human being was the sight of the kitchen table after Sara, Quentin, Jade and Karri (not their real names, but close) had finished preparing and eating their breakfast, and walked away.

I decided it was time for action. Two of the children – in fact the boys – agreed to light the wood stove, and the girls helped me fire up a starter mixture of flour, yeast and sugar, the basis for a dough.

We were to make pizzas for lunch.

It seemed inconceivable for my helpers – who thought chickens and eggs came from supermarkets – that you could actually make anything like a pizza in these spartan conditions, let alone using yeast. "Isn't that live or something?"

They were further surprised to learn you could make sweet as well as savoury pizzas, that a pizza could be baked that had the topping on the inside – the folded over Italian calzone – and that focaccia , which they thought was a trendy new bread, was simply another form of pizza, but coming from the north of Italy whereas pizza came from the south. As to the word itself, it amused them that pizza could have had its origins with the

Roman word placenta, a flat cake of flour, cheese and honey baked over hot ashes.

It was news to them that the French had a form of pizza called pissaladière , and they were astonished to learn that similar breads had been made in olden days in other parts of the world, for instance in England where they once baked 'trenchers', flat breads that were used as plates.

They liked the idea that the pizza dough would expand, that we would be proving it, but what most impressed them was how easy pizza was to prepare – and how inexpensive. Without power charges for cooking, around a dollar each one.

While the dough was rising, they grated cheese, sliced onions, cried, and screwed up their noses and chorused "yuk" when I suggested anchovies – which we agreed to put only on the adults' pizzas. They recommended pineapple and I screwed my nose up. We cut up salami, ham, mushrooms and capsicums, and we chopped herbs, oregano, rosemary and basil. For the sweet pizzas we washed grapes and sliced pears.

The new cooking team happily kneaded the dough, cut it into smaller pieces then worked it flat on the floured kitchen table (which I had had to scrub clean).

Then it was time to assemble the individual pizzas. Each teenager made up his and her own cheese and tomato topped pizza adding their own chosen ingredients.

Some pizzas had names on them, others had faces. We made a ham-and-cheese calzone, shaped like a pastie and filled with slices of ham, grated mozzarella, chopped oregano and black pepper.

Then we constructed a grape schiaccata, a pizza base topped with grapes and brown sugar with another pizza round placed on top, and a final dotting of grapes and brown sugar. The grapes on the inside would become soft and smooth, while those on top would be caramelised. And we prepared a pear pizza.

Then it was into the wood stove's oven, two pizzas at a time, to be baked in the heat of the roaring fire, cheesy, herby aromas filling the old building.

The whole thing was an experience for all, but perhaps the greatest wonder for me was the ingenuity displayed by the four new cooks. Just how did they manage to disappear without my noticing – just when it was time to clean up – only to reappear when the pizzas were cooked. Perhaps the parents were right and discovery learning was the way to go.

Whatever, the rewards were worth while. When the pizzas were served, new and more positive sounds had replaced the earlier gloom: "Mmmmmm", "Yum", "Cool", "Hot". Who could wish for more than that?

Guess who did the washing up!

A long weekend in the country with teenagers tested the tolerance of "this normally child-loving human". The photograph suggests tolerance may have been a two-way process at an earlier stage of life.

"Bread that has to be cut
with an axe is too nutritious."

FRAN LEBOWITZ

Bread

Sourdough Toastettes

On Consuming Passions master baker Kingsley Sullivan demonstrated how he makes his sourdough bread, the traditional way – with six-year-old sourdough mixture. But bought sourdough bread may be substituted, or any other good bread, come to that.

Serves 6

INGREDIENTS

6 medium tomatoes, very ripe
1 large loaf of sourdough bread
extra virgin olive oil
2 roasted capsicum, with
    skins removed
2 eggplant, sliced and roasted
    or barbecued
100g mature cheese
    (preferably goat cheese)
100g creamy young goat
    cheese (or cream cheese or
    creme fraiche)
fresh pepper to taste

METHOD

Slice the tomatoes and roast for one-and-a-half hours in the oven at 160°C.

Slice the loaf of sourdough bread diagonally into thick slices. Rub each slice on one side only with the olive oil. Top each slice with an assortment of the roasted tomato, capsicum and eggplant.

Then top with a mixture of the two types of cheese. Grind over some pepper. Put the slices on an oiled baking tray and roast in a very hot oven (230°-250°C) or grill until the cheese has softened and starts to bubble.

Olive Focaccia

Along with the olive and wine, bread and other wheat products have been the basis of the Mediterranean diet for centuries. This olive bread is a joy to make and works as well with dried yeast as it does with the fresh variety.

Makes 2 loaves

METHOD

Mix together 1 tablespoon white flour, the sugar, yeast and 2 tablespoons of the tepid water and stand for 20 minutes. This activates the yeast and the mixture should be frothy.

Mix the remaining white flour, the wholemeal flour and 1 tablespoon olive oil in a bowl. Add yeast mixture and remaining water and mix well. Cover with a damp tea towel and leave in a warm place for 1 hour.

Meanwhile, heat the remaining oil in a frying pan and cook onion over medium heat for 5 minutes, or until it softens. Stir in chopped olives and herbs and cook for about 30 seconds, then set aside.

Knead dough on a floured work surface for 5-6 minutes. Knead in olive/onion/herb mixture. (It doesn't matter if bits of olive fall out, just poke them back in).

Divide dough into two portions. Flatten each piece of dough into a fat pizza shape and put on an oiled pizza or baking tray. Cover with a damp tea towel and leave in a warm place for an hour or until risen.

Before baking, dimple surface of each loaf with your fingers, drizzle with a little more olive oil and scatter with additional olives. (Sprinkle with a little sea salt, if you like).

Bake at 200°C for about 25 minutes, or until top is golden brown and bottom is light brown.

Leftover potential: Does not keep well beyond a day.

INGREDIENTS

250g plain white flour

1 tsp sugar

1 x 7g sachet dried yeast

1½ cups tepid water

250g wholemeal flour

2 tbsp olive oil

1 medium onion, finely chopped

2 tbsp stoned and chopped olives (preferably black)

2 tbsp chopped fresh herbs of choice (preferably rosemary, parsley, oregano and thyme) or 1 tsp mixed dried herbs

additional plain flour for kneading

additional olives for final stage (these may be left unstoned)

Ricotta Calzone

A basic pizza dough encases a light, tasty mixture of ricotta cheese, parmesan cheese, sage, sun-dried tomatoes and anchovies.

Serves 6

INGREDIENTS

500g plain white flour plus
   2 tsp extra

1 tsp sugar

1 x 7g sachet dried yeast

1 tbsp extra virgin olive oil

500g ricotta cheese, drained
   to remove whey

2 tsp grated parmesan cheese

10 anchovy fillets (Australian
   if available), chopped

6-8 halves sundried or oven
   dried tomatoes, chopped

4 or 5 sage leaves (or 1 tsp
   dried sage), chopped

½ tsp ground black pepper

½ tsp grated nutmeg

METHOD

Mix together the 2 teaspoons flour, the sugar, yeast and 2 tablespoons of tepid water and stand for 15 minutes. This activates the yeast and the mixture should be frothy. Put all but a handful of the remaining flour into a large bowl. Add yeast mixture, oil and enough tepid water to make a firm dough. Cover bowl with a damp tea towel and leave in a warm place to prove for 1 hour.

In another bowl, mix together ricotta cheese, parmesan cheese, anchovies, tomatoes, sage, pepper and nutmeg.

Knead dough on a floured work surface for 8-10 minutes. Add more flour if dough sticks to your hands.

Divide dough into four portions. Roll each piece out to about 1cm thick and put on an oiled baking tray. Put one quarter of the cheese mixture on one side of each piece of dough and fold over the other side to make a pastie-like shape. Wet the edges with water. Press down along the semi-circle to seal, fold over edge and press again.

Bake at 220°C for 20 minutes or until top is beautifully browned.

Leftover potential: Best eaten immediately after cooking.

Hint: Brush the tops of the calzones with a little garlic-flavoured olive oil. The water used when activating the yeast should be no hotter than blood heat. Test the temperature with your finger – it should not feel warm.

Potato Pizza

A simple pizza style dish that doesn't need bread dough. It relies for its success on the humble spud. The recipe is for the base, which may be used to accompany other dishes, or you may add a pizza topping of your choice.

Serves 6

METHOD

Finely slice onions into rings and brown them in a little extra virgin olive oil. Once browned, add red wine. (Remember that if a wine's not worth drinking it's not worth cooking with.) Add thyme and reduce heat.

Leave onions to simmer in this mixture for about 40 minutes. Check from time to time to make sure they're not drying out too much and sticking to the pan. Just add a little wine to keep them moist. Peel and grate potatoes, squeeze in a tea towel to remove excess moisture.

In a large bowl, mix milk with the egg, flour, nutmeg, cheese and pepper. Add grated potato and onion mixture and stir well.

Oil a shallow pan which can be put in the oven. Pour the mixture into the pan.

Bake in oven at 200°C for about 40 minutes, after which time it should have started getting a golden crust.

At this stage, take it out and add some pizza toppings of your choice. Then put back into the hot oven or place it under the grill for a few moments.

Suggested topping: Tomato paste, anchovies, olives, capsicum, and low-fat mozzarella or bocconcini cheese.

INGREDIENTS

500g onions
2 tbsp extra virgin olive oil
1 cup red wine
2 tsp chopped fresh thyme or oregano (or ½ tsp chopped dried mixed herbs)
1 kg potatoes
2 tbsp reduced fat milk
1 egg
1 tbsp plain flour
½ tsp grated nutmeg
1 tbsp grated parmesan (or other hard cheese)
pepper to taste
pizza topping

"To get the best results, you must talk to your vegetables."

CHARLES, PRINCE OF WALES

Vegetables & Salads

Cheong Kahoona Pork Salad

One of the country's most influential chefs is Cheong Liew. This salad is an example of the simple way he combines ingredients to come up with sensational results.

Serves 6

INGREDIENTS

5 shallots, finely sliced (or 1 medium salad onion)
2 cloves garlic, chopped
1 tbsp olive oil
350g pork fillet, cut into thin strips across the grain
1 head of cos lettuce, leaves separated
1 ripe, but firm, pawpaw, peeled, seeded and cut into thin strips
$\frac{1}{4}$ cup pine nuts, toasted and sprinkled with a pinch of salt
2 tbsp chopped coriander leaves

Dressing

1 red chilli, seeded and finely chopped
(or 1 tsp chilli sauce)
2 cloves garlic, finely chopped
$\frac{1}{4}$ cup mirin (Japanese rice wine seasoning)
4 tbsp fish sauce
1 tbsp sugar

METHOD

To make dressing: Put all ingredients in a screwtop jar and shake well to dissolve sugar.

Pan-fry shallots and garlic in olive oil. Add pork and cook quickly over very high heat for about 30 seconds.

Arrange lettuce leaves on serving plates. Top with pork mixture and pawpaw, then sprinkle with dressing and garnish with pine nuts and coriander.

Leftover potential: Poor. Best eaten as soon as prepared.

Hint: To toast the pine nuts, put nuts in a dry frying pan over low heat and cook, shaking pan frequently, until lightly browned.

Lemony Mixed Vegetables

The perfect accompaniment to many meat dishes, the traditional mirepoix mixture of carrots, onions, leek and celery is cooked in wine and stock and served in a subtle lemon-flavoured sauce.

Serves 6

INGREDIENTS

2 leeks, finely sliced
4 tbsp good olive oil
2 medium onions, finely
 chopped
2 medium carrots, finely diced
2 sticks celery, finely diced
125ml dry white wine
125ml chicken, veal or
 vegetable stock
1$\frac{1}{2}$ tbsp lemon juice
4 egg yolks
2 tsp cornflour
$\frac{1}{2}$ tsp white pepper

METHOD

Into a heavy-based, deep saucepan, gently cook the leeks in the olive oil for 5 minutes, stirring frequently.

Stir in onions, carrots and celery and cook for about 2 minutes longer.

Add wine and stock, reduce heat and cook for a further 15 minutes.

Just before serving, whisk lemon juice with egg yolks, then stir in cornflour and white pepper.

Slowly stir 2 tablespoons vegetable liquid in egg yolk mixture. When well mixed, stir egg mixture into the vegetables to make a light lemon sauce.

Serving suggestion: Especially recommended as a partner for Herbed Lamb Balls (page 149).

Leftover potential: Keeps up to two days in the refrigerator.

Leek and Ham Gratin

A dish I learnt to prepare in Belgium. Pieces of cooked leek are wrapped in ham, then covered with a spicy cheese sauce. In Belgium, it is usually made with witloof (Belgian endive). I find the leek is a subtler alternative, without the bitterness which comes with the endive. The bed of mashed potatoes is optional but makes for a more substantial dish.

Serves 4

INGREDIENTS

4 leeks

3 tsp lemon juice

50g butter

50g plain flour

500ml milk

125g grated Swiss (or other) cheese

½ tsp grated nutmeg

¼ tsp paprika

2 tbsp chopped fresh parsley (optional)

1 egg yolk

mashed potato (optional)

200g lean ham slices

1 egg white

parmesan cheese

breadcrumbs

METHOD

Trim the leeks, removing the leafy top and the bottom. Cut a cross in the tops, plunge into cold water and soak to remove any soil.

Put leeks in a saucepan, cover with water, add 2 teaspoons lemon juice and simmer for about 30 minutes, or until cooked. Do not boil too rapidly or the leeks will break up.

Meanwhile, make a cheese sauce by melting the butter in a medium saucepan, then stir in the flour and cook gently for 3 minutes. Add the milk, a little at a time, stirring frequently, until sauce thickens. Stir in the cheese, nutmeg, paprika and parsley (if using).

When the cheese has melted and the sauce is smooth, remove from heat and whisk in egg yolk.

Drain the leeks well and cool a little before assembling the dish.

Spread a layer of mashed potato (if using), over the base of an ovenproof dish.

Roll leeks in ham slices, cutting the leeks into shorter lengths if they are too long. Place ham-wrapped leeks in the ovenproof dish and top with half the sauce.

Beat egg white with the remaining lemon juice until stiff peaks form. Fold egg white into the remaining sauce. Spoon over leeks, then sprinkle with parmesan cheese and a few breadcrumbs.

Bake at 190°C for 25-30 minutes or until top is beautifully browned.

Leftover potential: Keeps for two or three days in the refrigerator.

Leek and Ham Gratin

Filled Fungi

Filled Fungi

Who said 'life's too short to stuff mushrooms'? Actually I have said it, but I was referring to those little button mushrooms you find in cans. There is a great deal to be said for stuffing field mushrooms, as in this recipe. A topping of soft, young goat's cheese provides the finishing touch to this gastronomic delight.

Serves 4

METHOD

Remove stalks from mushrooms and chop them finely.

In a frying pan, gently sauté onion in 1 tablespoon olive oil for 5 minutes or until transparent. Add chopped mushroom stalks to pan and cook for 3 minutes longer.

Remove pan from heat and stir in nutmeg, ginger and salt and pepper. Add herbs, breadcrumbs, parmesan cheese and egg and mix gently.

Brush tops of mushrooms with a little olive oil. Turn them over and fill with herb mixture. Put on a baking tray and drizzle with a little of the remaining oil. Cover with foil or baking paper and bake at 180°C for approximately 25 minutes. (Check halfway through cooking to make sure mushrooms aren't looking dry. If they are, add a little more oil.)

Remove mushrooms from oven and top each with a couple teaspoons of goat cheese.

Serving suggestion: Serve warm with a rocket salad, lightly dressed with olive oil and balsamic vinegar.

Leftover potential: Keeps for a day in the refrigerator. Great served cold.

INGREDIENTS

4 large field mushrooms
1 large spanish (red) onion, finely chopped
2 tbsp extra virgin olive oil
$\frac{1}{4}$ tsp grated nutmeg
$\frac{1}{4}$ tsp ground ginger
salt and pepper to taste
2 tbsp chopped fresh herbs (I use parsley, thyme, oregano and a couple of leaves of sage or 2 tsp dried mixed herbs)
1 cup breadcrumbs (preferably made from day-old bread)
1 tbsp grated parmesan cheese
1 egg, lightly beaten
2 tbsp soft goat cheese (preferably Kervella)

LA Lore and a Big Apple

I did make one mistake, I asked an Afro-American waiter for a short black. I thought he was about to make me a flat white, but he fetched an espresso.

i suppose you could call it a culinary mission, maybe even the search for the Holy Quail. My quest: to check out what was happening with the East/West cuisine in the USA, in other words West Coast Californian and East Coast New York.

Preparations had been made and essential goods had been packed: passport, tickets, compass (always carried – well, you never know), adaptor plugs for foreign sockets, camera, an upside-down-under map of the world so I could keep my travels in perspective, an English-American dictionary (just kidding), and a corkscrew, that indispensable travel item for any gallivanting gourmand. I had consumed 500ml of carrot juice each day for five days prior to my departure – a method of avoiding jet lag used by some flight crews – and flew out of Sydney to Los Angeles.

Way to go...

A highlight of my visit to LA was a meeting with the head honcho of Bon Appétit magazine, the influential glossy which predicts and follows food trends, both in America and around the world. Probably creates a few, too.

I asked the Executive Editor, Barbara Fairchild about the trends in the US.

Preparations had been made and essentials packed.

"We have a sort of East Coast/West Coast dynamic happening here," she glowed, radiating enthusiasm. "Here on the West Coast, Asian cuisine is the thing. Five out of the seven new restaurants just opened in LA have Asian influences, principally Thai and

Vietnamese." Sounds familiar, doesn't it.

"At the same time, on the East Coast new restaurants are serving very large portions of meat and potatoes, specially steak. Home cooking around the country seems focused on Italian with grills and pasta being huge. Noodle restaurants are happening and chefs such as Mark Miller – of Coyote Cafe fame and known for his South-west American cuisine – is now opening a chain of Asian-style restaurants, such as Raku in Washington."

Sounds familiar again. By the way, Mark Miller is a regular visitor to Australia.

Ms Fairchild also sees a trend towards traditional techniques being taught by chefs and to a revival of fine dining.

And fine dining was certainly on the agenda that night at the imposing Four Seasons hotel in Beverley Hills.

This is one of those places where you're expected to be someone, but it doesn't really matter if you're not. As you enter the cocktail bar, everyone stops to look. Yes, everyone. Then, when it's realised you're not Madonna, Arnie, or Demi – and are never likely to be – they go back to their dry martinis, reputedly the best in California, if not the world.

It has to be said the restaurant is vain-friendly. With those at my table having trouble reading the menus – none was wearing glasses – the obliging Maitre d' brought across a fine wooden box containing an assortment of reading glasses for the diners to choose from. What a fine touch, I thought. And there were many takers at the table.

In the course of my flying visit I did make one big mistake, I asked an Afro-American waiter for a short black. I thought he was about to make me a flat white, but he was very charming about it and fetched me an espresso.

I tried to avoid any further gaffes as my host whizzed me around to a few of LA's more prominent restaurants. Just to get an overview.

We zoomed in and out of chef Wolfgang Puck's Spargo's II – well this is sequel town. This establishment was so new we had to gate-crash its opening party to check out its wood-fired ovens and glassed now-you-see-it kitchen. Then on to Dah Magreb (a restaurant right out of the Arabian Nights), Pinot (a very trendy CBD establishment, more wood-fired ovens and see-through kitchens), Chin Chin (very chic), Le Colonial (very Asian), Il Piccolini (not as small as it sounds), old Spargo's (a bit tatty with more burning wood but less glamour than the new one), Eclipse (where we couldn't actually see inside because the paparazzi were crowded round the doorway hoping for a glimpse of Joan Collins at an opening party), Il Fornaio (not Italian, but close), Le Dome (not very French) and Morton's. We managed to bolt down a little food here and there, and occasionally I had a glass of Californian Chardonnay or Cabernet Sauvignon, usually young and inexperienced. Along with the rest of LA, my host was sticking to his iced tea.

As I headed for the airport it occurred to me that foodwise Los Angeles is doing much of what we're seeing in Australia – only the portions are bigger. Generally the food is

"
I like to be in America. OK to be in America.
Everything free in America. For a small fee in America.
STEPHEN SONDHEIM *West Side Story*
"

good, mostly light with salsas rather than heavier sauces. Heaps of very good fish and seafood, but hardly any chicken is served in restaurants. Service is good, too, but you pay for it. Everything you see on a menu has what I call the plus-plus factor. A dish may appear to cost about the same as in Oz, but by the time you've added tax, service charge (in some cases up to 15 per cent) and the additional 'voluntary' tip – and if you're driving you will have paid for the ubiquitous valet parking, and the service on the valet parking – and unless you're into tea-drinking you'll be consuming wines at up to twice what you'd pay in Oz, you soon find you've bitten off more than you can chew! Next stop, New York.

The Big Apple

'Dawn in New York has four columns of mud and a hurricane of black doves wet from stagnant water,' wrote Federico Garcia Lorca back in 1930.

What it had for me was a hotel room that was smaller than the car from the airport, a view of Manhattan's darker side, and the sound of a large motor on the roof cutting in and out every six minutes. Things could only get better. Which, of course they did, after I had twice changed rooms.

But the food scene cheered me up no end.

Whether it's a market, a deli, a café or a grand eatery, New York has it in spades. Delis are big in the Big Apple. So big in fact that there is an entire vocabulary of deli terms, such that spare ribs are known as 'first lady', jello (or jelly to us) is 'nervous pudding', 'Adam's ale' is water, and 'clean up the kitchen' is hash. You get the picture?

And there are delis and delis, those of the magnificence of such landmarks as Dean and DeLuca or Balducci's – where the range of foods from around the world is mind-boggling

– to the mostly sit-down and fill-your-face affairs, such as the Carnegie Deli.

Carnegie's is not an establishment for the faint hearted – nor vegetarians, come to that. The location for part of Woody Allen's film, *Broadway Danny Rose*, this eatery is about meat, and lots of it. It's a place that not so much buzzes as crashes with activity. Plates groaning with food are banged unceremoniously on to tables. Orders are shouted out above the chatter.

Round the corner from the Carnegie Deli is the longest queue – 'line-up' in States talk – for food that I've ever seen. Apparently, every weekday, from midday exactly, owner Al Yeganeh serves soup to his dedicated patrons, most of whom take it back to their offices.

This is the International Soup Kitchen made famous by its portrayal in the Seinfeld TV show. Mr Yeganeh, whom the Seinfield team called the Soup Nazi because of his habit of not serving people he didn't like the look or sound of – could turn any international dish into a soup, whether it be moussaka or eggplant parmigiana. It has made this former physics student into a legend.

Foodism extends also to television in New York, where there is an entire cable network dedicated to it.

The TV Food Network occupies a whole floor of a tower block in Manhattan. It is here they make their own food programmes and screen other people's, and all with the kind of manic fervour that I was becoming used to in New York. I discovered scores of the food and wine obsessed working in the network's test kitchens, library, prop stores and transmission centres, poring over computers and microwaves. They even have a nightly food news bulletin. I kid you not, I made a brief appearance on it to talk about Australian food and wine.

And the trends...

Café style eating is as popular as in LA, or Sydney, Melbourne or any other Australian city, with typical NY fare.

At E.A.T. Café on Madison Avenue you could have such Jewish favourites as chicken soup with matzoh balls – those little savoury delights of which Marilyn Monroe is reported to have said: "Matzoh balls, always matzoh balls. Isn't there any other part of the matzoh you can eat?" – or gefilte fish. Then there's Beluga caviar omelette with field greens if you have $A70 to spare, and why not an accompanying '96 Meursault for a mere $A14. Cheap, you think? That's for a glass. And don't forget service is not included. Oh, and they only take American Express.

Then there's the trendy Union Square Café where their mashed turnips with crispy shallots are sensational, as is their creamy polenta with mascarpone, toasted walnuts and crumbled gorganzola, and the simmered white beans with herbs, pecorino and extra virgin olive oil are hard to resist – and they are just accompaniments, absolutely perfect with the crisp-roasted lemon-pepper duck with spicy apple pear chutney and wild rice pilaff.

For serious dining my three favourites were Nobu, Firebird and Chanterelle.

In style, Nobu is as close to Sydney's own Testsuya's as I have found. A strong Japanese influence here with dishes ranging from sea urchin tempura to New Zealand mussels with matsuhisa sauce and fresh lobster with wasabi pepper sauce.

Firebird is a Russian-inspired palace of gastronomy, grand and formal with fine dining rooms. Waiters (all men) wear Tsarist military-style uniforms in red and gold.

Chanterelle Restaurant's chef/owner David Waltuck has made his establishment one of those places worthy of a detour. Plenty of fish and seafood, mushrooms, some Japanese influences, and a tasting menu comprising an assortment of raw fish; an asparagus flan with fresh morels; 'diver caught' Maine sea scallops with duck fat, tomato and basil; breast of Muscovy duck with Chinese spices and sweet soya glaze; an assortment of cheese; and pineapple Kalamansi soup with yoghurt and lime sorbet.

Six courses, yours for $A120. A tasting of wines is a snip surely at just $A70 extra.

Both Los Angeles and New York regularly get their share of criticism, especially from Americans. Writer Tom Taussik says, "The difference between Los Angeles and yoghurt is that yoghurt has real culture." Of New York, Mignon McLaughlin: "A car is useless in New York, essential everywhere else. The same with good manners."

Certainly they're fast, they're brash, and they can be downright rude, but in the food and service departments you can get anything you want, for a small fee – plus, plus.

> *If food did not exist it would be well-nigh impossible to get certain types off the phone.*
>
> **FRAN LEBOWITZ** *Metropolitan Life* 1980

Warm Chicken Liver Salad

One of my all-time favourites adapted from French cuisine. Chicken livers, bacon and croutons are served with a lightly bitter curly endive and a sweet vinaigrette dressing. I use a Berry Farm pear vinegar, but any fruit vinegar or good balsamic vinegar will work.

Serves 4

INGREDIENTS

300g chicken livers

1 curly endive (or soft-leafed lettuce or salad mix)

3 tbsp olive oil plus 1 tbsp extra

1 tsp creamy dijon-style mustard

3 tsp fruit vinegar

2 tsp orange juice

2 cloves garlic, finely chopped or minced

2 slices white bread, crusts removed, cubed

4 rashers bacon, cut into 2cm wide strips

seasoned flour

spanish (red) onion, thinly sliced

METHOD

Clean chicken livers by removing sinews, then cut each into 2-3 pieces.

Wash endive in several changes of water to remove grit and reduce bitterness. Drain, tear into pieces and put into a salad bowl.

Make a vinaigrette by vigorously whisking I tablespoon of the olive oil with the mustard, vinegar, orange juice and garlic. Season to taste.

Heat remaining oil in a frying pan over high heat, add bread cubes and cook, tossing until brown. Remove and set aside.

Add bacon to pan and cook until crisp. Remove from pan, drain and set aside. Reserve fat in pan.

Toss chicken liver pieces in seasoned flour. Shake off excess flour and fry livers in pan used for cooking bacon and croutons, adding a little more oil if the pan is too dry. Take care not to overcook – they'll only need 1-2 minutes to be just cooked.

Scatter chicken livers, bacon and croutons over endive, drizzle over vinaigrette dressing and scatter with onion.

The liverless alternative: Instead of using chicken livers, poach an egg for each person and serve individual salads with a freshly poached egg on top of each. Use the same dressing.

Asparagus with Egg, Cream & Smoked Salmon Sauce

A perfect light entree for a summer's lunch or dinner, or it may be served as a light snack. For a less expensive dish, the smoked salmon can be omitted.

Serves 6 as entree

INGREDIENTS

500g fresh asparagus

3 eggs (any size)

25g butter

juice of $\frac{1}{2}$ lemon

1 tsp dijon mustard

150ml cream

100g smoked salmon

black pepper

dill (or other herb) to garnish

paprika or cayenne pepper to
    garnish (optional)

METHOD

Wash asparagus. Plunge them into boiling water and allow to cook for five or six minutes. They should still have a little crunchiness. Plunge into cold water and leave to cool. Drain.

Hard boil two of the eggs (about 7 minutes) and allow to cool in cold running water. Shell and chop finely.

Melt butter in saucepan. Add lemon juice and dijon mustard. Stir over low heat for 2 minutes.

Add cream and keep simmering while stirring so that the sauce reduces by about one-third.

Stir in the remaining egg (raw) and keep simmering over low heat until the mixture starts to thicken.

Remove from heat, stir in the chopped hard boiled egg and half the smoked salmon finely sliced.

Serve asparagus with remaining smoked salmon, sprinkle with black pepper, garnish with herbs and paprika (or cayenne pepper).

Note: I think this recipe works well with the asparagus served cold but the sauce still warm. The sauce could also be served cold.

Thai'd Up Prawn Salad

A light, but nourishing salad with a hint of chilli. A little sweet and sour miracle, that's made in no time and is wonderful served warm or cold.

Serves 4

INGREDIENTS

425g Australian canned peach slices, well drained
½ red capsicum
1 tsp sesame oil
small piece lemon grass stem, crushed and chopped (optional)
1 tsp finely chopped or minced ginger
2 tsp sweet chilli sauce
1 tbsp fish sauce (or reduced salt soya sauce)
1 tbsp lime or lemon juice
1 tbsp chopped coriander leaves
1 tbsp unsalted peanuts
750g large prawns, cooked and shelled
lettuce leaves (preferably a soft-leafed variety – but not iceberg!)
2 tbsp chopped spring onions
extra coriander leaves for garnish

METHOD

Dice one-third of peaches. Chop capsicum into small dice.

Heat sesame oil in a frying pan over medium heat, add lemon grass (if using) and ginger, and stir-fry for I minute.

Mix in chilli sauce, fish sauce and lime or lemon juice.

Mix capsicum and diced peaches with coriander leaves and ginger mixture.

In a frying pan over medium heat, lightly toast the peanuts. Add the prawns and cook, tossing, for a few seconds to warm. The prawns should not overcook.

Put lettuce leaves in a salad bowl, then add prawn and vegetable mixtures, toss and garnish with spring onions, remaining peach slices and extra coriander.

Serve slightly warm.

Leftover potential: Keeps for a couple of hours.

Thai'd Up Prawn Salad

Pat Cash Pasta Salad

The World's Best Chips

Spanakopita (Spinach Pie)

Spanakopita (Spinach Pie)

A wonderful blend of spinach with cheese and nuts, wrapped in filo pastry and baked. It's rich in vitamins A, C, E and it has some vitamin B for bliss! It also has so much iron, it's surprising it doesn't rust.

Serves 6

INGREDIENTS

1 bunch silver beet or spinach

1 chopped onion (red or white) or equivalent spring onions

1/2 cup ricotta cheese

60g fetta cheese

2 eggs

1/4 cup pinenuts (pecans or walnuts)

grated nutmeg

5 sheets filo pastry

olive oil

ground black pepper

METHOD

Strip the leaves from the stalks of the silver beet or spinach and chop finely.

Place spinach, onion, ricotta, fetta, eggs and pinenuts in a bowl and add nutmeg. Mix well.

Prepare filo pastry by brushing each sheet with a little olive oil sprinkling with black pepper between each sheet. Place each sheet on top of the other, leaving the top sheet unoiled and unpeppered.

Place the cheese mixture on to the edge of the pastry nearest you (try not to overload), then roll the mixture up so it finishes on its seam and fold in the edges.

Gently lift it on to an oiled tray and finally brush with olive oil and sprinkle with black pepper.

Place in a preheated oven 190°C-200°C and bake until it is brown, 40 to 45 minutes.

Pat Cash Pasta Salad

I created this recipe based on what Pat Cash told me were his favourite foods. Pat is a sportsman who takes his eating seriously – very little red meat, fats, oils or sugar. I used pumpkin pasta in the prototype but any pasta would do.

Serves 4

INGREDIENTS

1 tbsp olive oil
1 small eggplant, diced and
    pre-salted (see hint)
1 small zucchini, diced
1 young leek, finely sliced
juice of 1 orange
3 or 4 asparagus spears, cut
    in half
1/2 cup sugar snap peas or
    snow peas, trimmed
2 large ripe salad tomatoes
250g cooked pasta (preferably
    fettuccine or tagliatelle)
2 tbsp roasted hazelnuts
1 tbsp finely chopped basil
    leaves
1 tbsp finely chopped
    coriander leaves
1 tsp ground coriander

Dressing

2 tbsp lime or lemon juice
2 tsp sweet chilli sauce
1/2 tsp sesame oil

METHOD

Heat olive oil in a non-stick frying pan and stir-fry eggplant for about 5 minutes, or until softened.

Gently poach zucchini and leek slices in orange juice for 5 minutes. Drain.

Blanch asparagus and peas in boiling water for 30 seconds, then immediately transfer to cold water to set the colour.

Peel tomato, remove seeds and dice flesh finely. Place all salad ingredients in a salad bowl.

To make dressing: Whisk together lime or lemon juice, chilli sauce and sesame oil. Pour over salad and toss.

Leftover potential: Keeps a day in the refrigerator.

Hint: To prepare eggplant, sprinkle with salt and stand in a colander for at least 30 minutes. Rinse under cold water, drain, and dry on paper towels.

The World's Best Chips

METHOD

Peel potatoes and cut into strips no wider than a pencil (1cm). This is important! Wash well in cold water. Drain well and dry by shaking in a tea towel – or similar.

Heat oil to about 160°C. A chip dropped in it should float to the surface and bubble excitedly. Put in half the drained chip shapes. Cook until chips are soft and flexible – but not browned. Remove chips and drain.

Bring oil up to 160°C again and par-cook the remaining chips.

This procedure may be done anything up to six hours before the chips are needed.

Five minutes before serving bring the oil temperature up to 180°C. A chip dropped in it should float to the surface more excitedly than before.

Quickly cook half the cooled chips until they're a beautiful golden brown. A couple of minutes is all they should require. Drain well on kitchen paper.

Cook remainder and make a start eating the first batch while the second lot are draining.

Note: My mother kept a chip pan with vegetable or nut oil which was used several times before being discarded. This practice has been criticised as being unhealthy, however, it's practised by most restaurants and take-away outlets. Most outlets these days advertise using cholesterol free oil. Be aware that the oil used is often palm oil, which is high in saturated fat. By cooking chips yourself you can guarantee the ingredients are the best quality.

Handy tip: Make sure chips do not overcrowd the oil and that you allow for some frothing of the oil. Take care it does not spill over. If the potatoes are really dry you will minimise the risk of boil over.

There is no doubt that the world's best chips – or french fries – are in fact made in Belgium, though the Dutch might dispute this. Chips, Belgian-style, are the first dish I learned to make at the age of nine. And to go with them I like to make my own mayonnaise using dijon mustard, an egg yolk, wine vinegar and olive oil mixed to a creamy consistency in the blender. A mayonnaise recipe may be found on page 89 (omit coriander). Because take-away and restaurant chips are so often disappointing, I offer you this recipe for do-it-yourself potato chips which are guaranteed to be superb.

INGREDIENTS

1 kg potatoes
large quantity of oil in large
   pan (look for an oil low in
   saturated fat)

Roasted Toms

Now that sun-dried tomatoes have become passé, here's a great alternative – tomatoes slow-roasted in the oven with herbs. I like to use the hardy herbs such as thyme, rosemary and oregano. They are rich in oils and are usually in plentiful supply. They are discarded after use.

INGREDIENTS

1 kg ripe tomatoes
2 tbsp extra virgin olive oil
1 tbsp raw sugar
1 tsp black pepper
bunches of thyme, rosemary
    and oregano

METHOD

Lightly oil a baking tray.

Cut tomatoes in half and place cut side up on the prepared tray. Drizzle tomatoes with olive oil and sprinkle with sugar and pepper.

Top tomatoes with generous amounts of herbs – it's really hard to overdo it.

Roast at 150°C for at least one-and-a-half hours. Serve hot from the oven, or cold in salads.

Leftover potential: Roasted tomatoes keep for two or three days in the refrigerator.

Seafood Salad with Coriander Mayonnaise

This dish was created in honour of the men and women on board 'HMAS Darwin'. I used a range of seafoods from around the country, from Fremantle sardines to Tasmanian salmon and Sydney rock oysters, but any combination will work well. It's the lime and coriander that makes it such a huge success.

INGREDIENTS

1-2 kg assorted ready-to-eat
  seafood (depending on
  type. You'll need more if
  using lots of shellfish)

Coriander Mayonnaise
2 egg yolks
grated rind and juice of
  2 sweet limes (or 1 lemon)
2 tsp dijon-style mustard (or a
  mild Australian mustard)
pinch salt
½ tsp white pepper
1 tsp sesame oil
500ml light oil (olive, canola,
  peanut or macadamia)
2 tsp chopped coriander
  leaves
sugar (optional)

METHOD

To make mayonnaise: Put egg yolks into a bowl, then whisk in lime rind and juice, mustard, salt and pepper. Gradually whisk in sesame oil, a drop at a time. Slowly whisk in remaining oil, increasing the amount you add each time once the mixture starts to thicken. Stir in coriander. You may need to add a little sugar if the citrus juice is too sour.

Serving suggestion: Put mayonnaise in a bowl and arrange with seafood on a large serving platter.

Leftover potential: The mayonnaise keeps for a couple of days in an airtight container in the refrigerator. Because it contains raw egg, it shouldn't be stored any longer.

Chicken Potato Salad

A classic of Turkish cuisine from the days of the Ottoman Empire, when it could have been served in the harem. This is a delightful dish which has been given an updated Australian treatment using potatoes.

Serves 4

INGREDIENTS

500g potatoes (pontiacs are ideal)
1 litre chicken stock
1 small onion spiked with 3 or 4 cloves
2 sprigs thyme (or ½ tsp dried)
2 chicken breast pieces, skinned
2 slices bread, crusts removed
1 small onion, grated
1 clove garlic, crushed
50g pecan nuts, finely chopped (or walnuts)
1 cup finely chopped parsley or basil
few lettuce leaves
2 tbsp extra virgin olive oil (or macadamia nut oil)
2 tsp paprika

METHOD

Wash potatoes, cut into cubes (with skins still on) and poach in chicken stock.

Add clove-studded onion, the thyme and the chicken breasts and let the breasts poach slowly with the potatoes for 15 minutes.

Meanwhile, soak bread in stock, squeeze out excess. In a bowl, crumble bread, add grated onion, garlic, nuts and herbs. Mix thoroughly adding a little chicken stock to make a smooth paste.

When chicken breasts are cooked, remove from stock and allow to cool. Chop finely and add to nut mixture. This process could be done in a food processor for a smoother mixture. When potatoes are cooked, remove from stock, drain and allow to cool.

To assemble salad: Place a few lettuce leaves on a serving plate, add potato cubes and spoon over the chicken nut mixture.

Heat olive oil, add paprika and heat for a minute. Drizzle this oil/paprika mixture over salad.

Note: The stock may be used again. Simply remove the clove-studded onion and store stock in the refrigerator or deep freeze.

Garlic French Beans

*A deliciously gallic –
as well as garlic – way
of serving french
beans (also known
as stringless or
crawler beans).*

Serves 6

INGREDIENTS

500g French beans
1 clove garlic, finely chopped
   or pressed
2 tsp extra virgin olive oil
pepper to taste

METHOD

Wash, top and tail beans. Plunge into lots of boiling water and cook on rapid boil for five or six minutes. (They should still be crunchy but not taste raw.) Drain and plunge them immediately into cold water. Drain again.

In same pan, over low heat, stir garlic into olive oil for 30 seconds. Stir in beans until they are well coated with the oil and the garlic.

Season to taste and serve.

Leek and Mushroom Terrine

Serves 8

INGREDIENTS

2 leeks

2 medium carrots

12 stringless beans, topped
and tailed

6 or 7 tsp powdered gelatine

½ litre canned chicken or
beef consomme

200g mushrooms

½ tbsp olive oil

½ tsp grated nutmeg

1 hard boiled egg, sliced

1 sprig oregano or parsley, to
garnish

5 or 6 strips of roasted
capsicum, optional

METHOD

Clean leeks and boil about 30 minutes in lots of water.

Finely slice carrots, lengthwise. Boil for five or six minutes. Cook stringless beans for a couple of minutes then plunge them into cold water so they keep their colour. Allow all vegetables to cool.

Sprinkle the gelatine into the warmed stock, stirring all the time to make an aspic.

Slice mushrooms and sauté in olive oil for two or three minutes over high heat; sprinkle with nutmeg. Once all the vegetables are cold you may fill the terrine.

Use an earthenware dish, preferably a glazed rectangular dish (or terrine). Smear a little oil on bottom and sides.

Put hard boiled egg pieces on the bottom of the dish and some mushroom pieces and the herb garnish. When it's turned out of the dish, this layer helps the presentation.

Now tear the leeks apart and lay strips over the mushroom and egg pieces. Add a layer of carrot, some beans, capsicum and pour over some aspic mixture to cover. Repeat the process until all vegetables are used up.

Pour over a final drop of aspic mixture. Refrigerate overnight. The terrine should be as cold as possible.

To turn out, stand dish in hot water for a minute or so, to melt aspic at the sides and bottom.

Turn dish upside down over serving plate and lift dish clear (all being well). If it proves difficult to extract, slide a knife down the sides of the dish and repeat.

Nashi Cheese Salad

A great way of stretching a fabulous cheese a long way in this lovely summer's luncheon dish. The cheese is served with nashi fruit, celery, capsicum and nuts along with a dressing of mango, olive oil, balsamic vinegar and dijon mustard.

Serves 6

INGREDIENTS

250g ripe Australian soft
   ripened cheese
   (brie, camembert)
100g chopped macadamia
   nuts (or almonds, hazelnuts
   or pecans)
1 bunch english spinach, well
   washed
1 stick celery, cut finely
2 tbsp red or yellow capsicum,
   finely sliced
50g cherry tomatoes
1 large nashi, cubed
1 mango
2 tsp dijon mustard
2 tbsp good wine vinegar,
   preferably balsamic
2 tbsp extra virgin olive oil

METHOD

Cut the cheese into bite-sized pieces and roll in the chopped nuts.

Put spinach leaves in large mixing bowl. Add celery, capsicum, cherry tomatoes and nashi. Mix together.

Cut flesh from mango. Cut one half into slices and put into salad. Mash other half of mango in separate mixing bowl and stir in mustard, vinegar and olive oil. Mix well.

Pour dressing over salad and toss well. Put salad into serving dish. Dot with nut-coated cheese cubes. Sprinkle over remaining nuts.

Belgium's Rich Tradition

My child's paradise was Le Bouquet Romain, a sit-down café where ice-creams were the only dishes served. There were 35 different combinations.

thank goodness for cookbooks. When you're in Belgium at least you can read about good food.' This pejorative pronouncement – attributed to French writer Charles Beaudelaire – gives an indication of the contempt in which Belgian cuisine has been held by some Europeans, notably by the Belgians' neighbours, the French to the south and the Dutch to the north.

Perhaps because of the Belgians' natural conservatism and reserve, little is widely known of what is produced in this tiny country, and there are few Belgian restaurants in other parts of the world to demonstrate the nation's culinary flair. And flair they certainly have.

Growing up in Brussels, my earliest memories were of the superb pâtés and terrines, the hams, bacons and sausages, the marzipan fruits at Christmas time, the swan-shaped choux pastries filled with fresh cream on Sundays, the waffles topped with fresh cream, the ice-creams – also topped with cream – deep-fried apple beignets (fritters), the superb combination of twice-cooked chips and mayonnaise and of course, the chocolates, which are the world's finest.

In those indulgent days my child's paradise was Le Bouquet Romain, in the centre of Brussels, a sit-down café establishment where ice-creams were the only dishes served. There were 35 different combinations, the most popular being the Dame Blanche – or white lady, comprising a mountain of vanilla ice-cream smothered with hot Belgian chocolate sauce, topped with whipped cream, sprinkled with nuts and served with a really crisp sugary wafer biscuit.

If by now you get the impression that Belgian food is rich, you are absolutely right. Traditionally most savoury dishes are cooked in butter, and some restaurants boldly display 'cuisine au beurre' to indicate they do not substitute with margarine.

Chips are served with everything, even with mussels cooked 'mariniere' with wine, shallots, celery, parsley, lemon, and egg yolks. Soups and casseroles are taken very seriously, the Waterzooi of chicken from Flanders being perhaps the most popular. Made of chicken and vegetables seasoned with lemon, nutmeg, bay and thyme, in a sauce thickened with a mixture of egg yolks and cream, this dish is usually served as a cross between a soup and a casserole. My own version tends to be more of a casserole consistency and has been modified to make it less rich.

The Belgians are prodigious beer drinkers, who once held the dubious distinction of having the world's highest per capita consumption. Apparently the Belgians have now been overtaken by the Germans.

Beer has been part of Belgian society since

Roman times and is used extensively in the cooking, in batters and in stews such as the classic Carbonnades Flamandes, beef simmered in beer.

Game has always been popular, though some of the old recipes such as Liege-style thrush, woodcock mousse and leg of wild boar have been falling by the wayside as the country becomes increasingly industrialised. And seafood is always a feature of a restaurant menu, a typical entree being tomatoes stuffed with a mixture of tiny Ostend shrimps and real egg mayonnaise.

While having a wide range of meat and fish concoctions, Belgians also take pride in their vegetable dishes, notably made with the fat white asparagus of Malines, leeks, Brussel sprouts – of course – potatoes, celeriac, and Belgian endive. This slightly bitter shoot vegetable, that has been described as being like a corn on the cob, but with all husk and no cob, has soared in popularity outside Europe in recent years, and has been the source of some minor confusion around the world, not helped by the Belgians having two languages, French and Flemish. In Flemish the vegetable is witloof and in French chicon. It is also known as chicory.

The country's two languages used to lead to some curious experiences for tourists driving through it, such as where the town of Malines on your French-produced Michelin map turns out to be called Mechelen when you get there. And Liege is called Luik in Flemish. And

A young Ian Parmenter with Louise, Belgian housekeeper and early culinary influence.

Antwerpen is Anvers. You get the idea? Nowadays dual signage has helped.

During the last 30 years Belgium, and particularly Brussels, has changed out of sight. In the 1960s it acquired acronyms and the bulky bureaucracies that inevitably go with them. They got the EEC, NATO and SHAPE and the locals got higher prices in the restaurants. The long lunch, the traditional main meal of the day where citizens would go home from work or school, began to disappear.

On my last visit I was shocked to find that many of Brussels' restaurants had closed by 9pm and many others had changed to suit the international palates. Slow food had moved over as fast food had moved in. There were still a few superb traditional rotisseries near the Grand Place, but with prices reflecting the changing times.

Thank goodness for Belgian cookbooks!

> " *I never worry about diets. The only carrots that interest me are the number you get in a diamond.* "
>
> **MAE WEST** *The Wit and Wisdom of Mae West* 1967

Hayman Pasta Salad

A creation of Dieter Grün, formerly executive chef at the Hayman Island resort in Queensland, now in charge of the kitchens at Homebush's Olympic stadium. He has cooked the noodles in stock for added flavour but you can cook them in salted water, if you prefer.

Serves 4

INGREDIENTS

200g dried egg noodles
chicken stock (or salted water)
extra virgin olive oil
400g beef fillet
2 medium tomatoes
1 cucumber, peeled
1 cos lettuce
1 tbsp chives or spring onions, chopped (for garnish)

Dressing

2 tbsp chopped mint leaves
2 tbsp chopped coriander leaves
1 lime
2 tbsp sweet thai-style chilli sauce
2 tbsp extra virgin olive oil
salt and pepper to taste

METHOD

Cook the noodles in a large quantity of stock, or water. (If using stock, it can be re-used after the noodles have been cooked). Drain and toss in a little olive oil.

Slice the beef fillet into 1cm slices, across the grain.

To make the dressing: Mix together the mint, coriander, grated lime rind, lime juice, sweet chilli sauce, olive oil, and salt and pepper to taste.

Dice the tomato flesh and the peeled cucumber, discarding seeds. Wash the lettuce, drain and dry. Put a bed of lettuce, cucumber, tomato and some of the noodles on to individual plates.

Sear the beef fillet slices in a very hot frying pan smeared with a little olive oil, a few seconds each side.

While the meat is still warm, toss in the dressing, then arrange the slices over the noodles on the plate.

Serve immediately garnished with the chives or spring onions.

Leftover potential: Best eaten immediately, but it could be eaten cold the next day.

Wine choice: I like a pinot noir with this dish.

Andrew Fielke's Brioche with Mushrooms

A delightful recipe which can be made quickly if you are using bought brioche.

Serves 4

METHOD

To make the brioche: Mix the milk, yeast and sugar together. Put in a warm place and allow to prove for 15 minutes.

Mix together the flour, egg yolks, and melted butter with the yeast mixture. Stir in the chopped pepper berries and work into a smooth dough (adding more flour if the mixture is too sloppy). Cover loosely with plastic cling-wrap and allow to prove until it has doubled in size. Then knead well. Divide the pastry into four equal portions, removing a small piece from each one for the brioche top.

Put each large piece of brioche dough into a greased brioche tin. Roll each small piece into a cone shape. Make a small impression in the top of the brioche and insert the cone-shaped tops. Glaze with the egg yolk and milk mixture.

Bake at 190°C for 15 minutes, or until nicely browned.

To make the mushrooms: Melt the butter in a pan, stir in the mushrooms and allow to cook over a medium heat. Add the greens (or spinach) and stir to warm through. Keep in a warm place.

To make the beurre rouge: Put the shallots in a non-stick pan with the wine, balsamic vinegar and pepper berries. Reduce this liquid by a third. Slowly add the butter cut into cubes, stirring all the time over a medium heat.

When the mixture has become smooth and creamy, serve with the hot brioche and mushrooms.

INGREDIENTS

Brioche
2 tbsp milk, tepid
14g or 15g dried yeast
1 tbsp sugar
190g plain flour
2 egg yolks
125g unsalted butter, melted
1 tbsp chopped Tasmanian
    pepper berries
additional flour for kneading
glaze of 2 tbsp milk and
    1 egg yolk

Mushrooms
1 heaped tsp unsalted butter
150g mixed mushrooms (such
    as shiitake, abalone, field,
    and oyster)
150g warrigal greens (or
    spinach), blanched briefly
    in boiling water

Beurre rouge sauce
2 tsp chopped shallots
1 glass red wine (such as
    pinot noir)
1 tbsp balsamic vinegar
2 tsp Tasmanian pepper
    berries, chopped finely
100g unsalted butter
salt and pepper to season

"Fish, to taste right,
     must swim three times – in
water, in butter and in wine."

POLISH PROVERB

fish & seafood

Ginger Fish Sauna

One of my favourite ways of dealing with a whole fish. It's steamed over a spicy ginger liquor, which then becomes a tasty sauce.

Serves 4

INGREDIENTS

1 whole fish (coral trout, snapper) about 1.5 kg, cleaned and scaled

1 tbsp turmeric

1 x 5cm piece of ginger, crushed

juice and pared rind of 1 orange

750ml fish or chicken stock

1 tbsp reduced salt soya sauce

3 cardamom pods, crushed

1 tsp chopped or minced ginger

1 tsp minced chilli

2 tsp peanut butter

2 tbsp coconut milk (optional)

1 tbsp chopped spring onions, white part only

¼ capsicum, cut into thin strips

1 tbsp peanuts

1 tsp sesame oil

1 tbsp chopped spring onions, green part only

METHOD

Pat fish dry with paper towels. Cut a few slashes in the fish on each side. Place turmeric in a plastic bag and shake to distribute evenly. Put fish in the bag and shake to cover with turmeric. Remove fish from bag. Place the crushed ginger and orange rind in body cavity.

In a wok large enough to hold the fish, put the orange juice, stock, soya sauce, cardamom pods, chopped or minced ginger and chilli.

Put chopsticks across the wok to hold the fish – or you could use a wire rack. Place the fish on the chopsticks or rack. Cover with lid or aluminium foil and steam for 30-40 minutes. Remember to allow longer if the fish has come directly out of the refrigerator.

To check if fish is cooked, insert a knife into the flesh. When it flakes and comes away from the bone, it is cooked. When cooked, removed the fish from the wok and put in a warm place.

Remove rack from wok and cook steaming liquor to reduce to one-third of its volume. Remove cardamom pods. Stir in the peanut butter and coconut milk (if using) and heat. Do not allow the mixture to boil once the coconut milk is added. Briefly fry white parts of spring onions, capsicum and peanuts in the sesame oil. Serve fish topped with sauce, capsicum mixture and green parts of spring onions.

Serving suggestion: Delicious served with boiled brown rice and stir-fried vegetables.

Leftover potential: Best eaten immediately, or cold the same day.

Ginger Fish Sauna

Shandrani Fish and Eggplant

Lime and Ginger Fish Parcels with Citrus Sauce

Orange Prawns with Noodles

Orange Prawns with Noodles

Due to the acidity of the sauce, make it in a non-reactive pan.

Serves 4

INGREDIENTS

750ml orange juice

750ml low-salt fish or chicken
   stock

2 tsp wine vinegar

2 tbsp finely chopped carrot

2 tbsp finely chopped celery

2 tbsp finely sliced leek

2 tbsp finely chopped onion

500g large green prawns in
   their shells

1 tbsp olive oil

1 x 375g packet egg noodles,
   boiled but still al dente

pepper to taste

METHOD

In a large, non-reactive saucepan, put orange juice, stock, wine vinegar and 1 tablespoon of each of the carrot, celery, leek and onion. Reserve the rest for later use. Cook the vegetables over medium heat for 25 minutes.

Meanwhile, peel the prawns and put the shells and heads in the pan with the vegetables so that they contribute their flavour. Once all have been peeled, cut along the back of each prawn and remove the dark intestinal tract, rinse and dry on paper towels.

Cook prawns lightly in olive oil for about 1 minute. They don't need to cook right through at this stage and it is important the prawns aren't overcooked. Transfer to a warm place.

Strain stock mixture, discarding the prawn shells, heads and vegetables.

Return strained stock to the pan, add remaining vegetables and cook until the stock mixture reduces and is of a syrupy consistency, and the vegetables are softened. Remove pan from the heat. Stir in the prawns and the freshly cooked, but still warm, noodles. Season to taste.

Leftover potential: May be reheated the same day, but I wouldn't recommend keeping it beyond that.

Shandrani Fish and Eggplant

An unusual partnership, fish with eggplant, prepared by Creole chef Jean-Claude Michel at the Hotel Shandrani Blue Bay, Mauritius.

Serves 8

INGREDIENTS

1 kg white fish fillet (such as snapper, dhufish or red emperor) cut into 4cm cubes

2 tbsp olive oil

1 large or 2 medium eggplants, peeled and cut into 4cm cubes

1 medium onion, finely chopped

1 tsp grated or minced garlic

1 tsp grated or minced ginger

200g chopped fresh or canned tomatoes

3 tsp tomato paste

1 tbsp finely chopped parsley

1 tbsp finely chopped chives (optional)

2 tsp finely chopped fresh thyme (or ½ tsp dried thyme)

1 tbsp finely chopped coriander leaves

METHOD

In a frying pan (preferably non-stick) or wok, sauté fish, a few cubes at a time, in a little oil for 2-3 minutes or until almost cooked. It should be almost opaque – it is important not to overcook the fish. Add more oil as necessary to prevent fish sticking. Remove and keep warm.

Sauté eggplant in remaining oil for 8-10 minutes or until soft – eggplant should not be undercooked.

Add onion, garlic and ginger and cook for 2-3 minutes. Add tomatoes, tomato paste and herbs and return eggplant to pan. Simmer for 5 minutes over low heat.

Stir in fish and cook for 1-2 minutes longer or until fish is cooked through. Season to taste.

Serving suggestion: Serve with rice, grated carrot and cucumber, sweet chilli sauce and sweet mango chutney.

Leftover potential: Best eaten immediately after cooking.

Lime and Ginger Fish Parcels with Citrus Sauce

Another fish parcel recipe, which may be prepared with salmon, tuna or any white fish fillets.

Serves 4

INGREDIENTS

oil for brushing baking paper
4 x 150g fish fillets
4 spring onions, finely
   chopped
1 red or yellow capsicum,
   seeded and thinly sliced
2 tsp finely sliced ginger
2 tsp grated lime rind
1 tbsp lime juice
2 tsp sesame oil
1 tbsp soya sauce (preferably
   tamari)
white pepper

Citrus Sauce

1 tbsp lime juice
4 tbsp fish stock
4 tbsp port or muscat
1 tsp finely chopped ginger
1 tsp grated lime peel
2 tsp finely chopped onion
1 tsp cornflour mixed with 1
   tbsp water

METHOD

Cut four pieces of non-stick baking paper big enough to wrap each fillet separately and brush with a little oil. Put a fillet on one side of each piece of paper and top each with spring onions, capsicum, ginger, lime rind, lime juice, sesame oil, soya sauce and pepper.

Fold paper over and roll edges to seal. Put parcels on a baking tray and bake at 180°C for 15 minutes or until just cooked.

Meanwhile, make the sauce. Put all the sauce ingredients, except the cornflour mixture, into a saucepan. Bring to the boil over medium heat and boil for 2-3 minutes to reduce and blend the flavours. Remove from heat, stir in cornflour mixture and cook, stirring, until sauce thickens.

Serving suggestion: Open parcels at table and spoon over a little sauce.

Leftover potential: May be eaten cold the following day.

Delicious Mauritius

"Have it, it's on the house," the stallholder told me. "It's an aphrodisiac. Grate a little into some boiling water. Drink, and at night, paradise."

I didn't really know what I'd find when I got to Mauritius. I knew what I wouldn't find: the dodo. That hapless and ungainly bird was eaten out of existence by the island's first settlers, the Dutch, who first occupied Mauritius in 1558, gave it its name – after Prince Maurice of Nassau – and stayed until the early 18th century, when they were driven away by cyclones and plagues of rats. (I'm sure the dodo would have approved.)

I did know that, hidden from Africa by Madagascar and kept from the rest of the world by the Indian Ocean, Mauritius remained undiscovered until the Arab traders made it their trans-oceanic stopover around 1,000 years ago. Or it could have been the Malays who got there first. No-one seems sure.

So what is Mauritius today, and where does its gastronomy come from?

First, it is a country of paradoxes. The official language is English, though Creole or French is more often used conversationally. Driving is on the left on the roads that appear to be retreats for old Austin Cambridges, and the road signs are very old English, even down to the quaint 'Halt at Major Road Ahead'.

As to the people, of its one million population, it's reckoned that fewer than 10,000 are of European descent, and most of them are descended from the French.

The majority of the population are descended from settlers from India, mainly from Bihar and Tamil Nadu. They make up 700,000, while the rest are mostly Creoles, by definition of mixed descent, African and European – and Chinese. The multi-racial mix is reflected in the diet, which is based on rice. Tomatoes, onions, garlic, chillies and ginger feature prominently along with seafoods.

Palm hearts, wild boar and venison also make frequent appearances, but usually on the plates of the better-healed. An upmarket national dish is a salad of fresh palm-hearts and camarons, the local prawns. It is appropriately named 'Millionaire's Salad'.

While the French influence is still firmly planted in Mauritian haute cuisine, the dishes have been adapted for the climate. Among the most popular are rougaille, a substantial spicy tomato-based ragout seasoned with the ground heads and shells of tiny river prawns and usually served with fish. Then there's vindaye, a fish dish made with saffron, onions and garlic, mustard seeds and vinegar. Both are named after the French for garlic, ail.

Because of the large numbers of visitors from Northern Europe – predominantly France and Germany – dishes often are served lightly spiced along with accompaniments, achards – vegetables or fruits pickled in vinegar and seasoned with mustard seeds – and the hottest of chilli sauces. It allows individual diners to play with their food and turn up the heat as it suits them.

Breads range from French baguette to Indian purris, made with wheat, or dholl purris made with lentils and thefarata, a kind of damper.

Not surprisingly, the desserts reflect the importance sugar plays in the island economy. Ninety per cent of Mauritius' land mass is given over to sugar production, and whether the final result is sugar itself, pastries, confectioneries or the classic Mauritian Green Island Rum, much of it is consumed here, along with coconut and tropical fruits.

Snacks, called gajaks, range from Indian samosas to Chinese spring rolls.

Local food certainly is not confined to the locals. Most hotels and resorts recognise that today's holidaymaker is not looking for 'international' hotel cuisine as much as a chance to try indigenous dishes.

More often than not, dinners are served to the accompaniment of the Sega (pronounced Say-Grr), a percussive form of African music performed by drummers and dancers beside a raging bonfire on the beach.

As to drinks, Mauritian food in restaurants is often served with Phoenix, the island's malty beer, rather than the imported wines, which tend to be overpriced. I was advised to take my own wines with me and I did just that. The local rum makes for an excellent aperitif, especially when mixed with fresh fruit juices, rather than overpowering colas.

All in all, whether breakfasting or dining, the fare is always a taste and texture sensation, reflecting the colourful, sunny natures of the people, whose friendliness and kindness is beyond compare.

Not once did I hear the familiar and insincere 'have a nice day'. The warm welcome is felt everywhere, in shops, restaurants and markets, especially the markets where an interest in the produce is enough to provoke beaming smiles.

It was here I experienced a real 'moment' of generosity when the veteran holder of a stall specialising in herbal remedies – "everything treated from cellulite to cholesterol" – offered me a stick of wood.

"Have it, it's on the house," he said. "It's an aphrodisiac. Grate a little into some boiling water. Drink, and at night, paradise."

I'll probably never know if it works. It was confiscated by customs and quarantine staff when I returned to Australia. I hope they put it to good use!

Mauritius, a country full of paradoxes, exotic foods and quaint traffic conditions.

Fish and Asparagus with Five Spice Hokkien Noodles

This is one of the quickest dishes to prepare. Fish fillets are pan-fried and served in a light spicy sauce on a base of noodles. Hokkien noodles can be bought ready-cooked in most supermarkets and oriental food stores. You may use fettuccine instead, if you prefer.

Serves 4

INGREDIENTS

400g fresh asparagus
4 white fish fillets (approx.
    150g each)
400g cooked hokkien noodles
1 tbsp oil for frying
2 tbsp chopped fresh
    coriander leaves

Sauce

3 tbsp lemon juice
grated rind of a lemon
1 tbsp water
$\frac{1}{4}$ tsp five spice
$\frac{1}{4}$ tsp white pepper
1 tbsp fish sauce
1 generous tbsp honey
1 tbsp light soy sauce
$\frac{1}{4}$ tsp ground ginger (or 1 tsp
    minced ginger)

METHOD

Trim and wash the asparagus. Cook for 4-8 minutes depending on the thickness. Drain and keep warm on a paper towel. Pan-fry the fish fillets for 2-3 minutes each side (or more depending on thickness). Remove from the pan and keep warm.

To make the sauce: Mix all the ingredients together.

Put the sauce mixture into the frying pan used for the fish and cook over a medium heat for 2-3 minutes, allowing it to reduce.

Plunge the noodles into boiling water for 1-2 minutes to reheat. Toss the sauce through the noodles.

Place the noodles on to individual plates. Cover with the drained asparagus, top with the fish fillet and garnish with fresh coriander.

Barbecued Sardines

In the past we non-Mediterraneans usually thought of sardines as oily little things packed shoulder-to-shoulder in tiny flat tins with keys that either broke or got lost. Fortunately, the tide has turned and we are now able to get freshly caught sardines in Australian waters. In the absence of sardines, this dish may be prepared with other small, freshly caught fish.

Serves 4

INGREDIENTS
12 -16 sardines (approx. 750g)
black pepper
2 cloves garlic, finely chopped
1 tbsp olive oil
Juice of 2 lemons
1 tsp grated lemon rind
12 fresh basil leaves

METHOD
Clean the sardines by cutting a small incision along the belly and scooping out the innards with your finger.

Rinse the fish thoroughly under cold running water and drain. Pat dry with paper towels.

Sprinkle the fish with the pepper and garlic. Toss with the olive oil. Let sit for 15 minutes, turning once. Barbecue the sardines a couple of minutes each side.

Serve sprinkled with lemon juice and rind, some more pepper and the fresh basil.

Citrus Chilli Fish

This is a simple East meets West type of dish and celebrates the freshness, vitality and diversity of food in Australia. In the recipe I have used only lemon, however cumquats, grapefruits and limes can be used. I add saffron for colour and flavour, but it is expensive and may be omitted.

Serves 4

INGREDIENTS

1 medium zucchini
1 small onion, finely chopped
2 tbsp extra virgin olive oil
1 tsp finely chopped garlic
1 tsp finely chopped ginger
750ml fish or chicken stock
juice and rind of 1 lemon
2 tbsp sweet thai chilli sauce
1 heaped tsp sugar
1 tsp saffron strands
   (optional)
1¼ cups long grain rice
4 thick fillets of white fish
   such as snapper, red
   emperor, perch (approx.
   750g each)
2 tbsp chopped fresh
   coriander leaves

METHOD

Peel the zucchini lengthwise. Cut the peel into julienne strips. Set the peel aside. Remove the flesh from the central core. Cut the zucchini flesh into dice-size pieces.

Gently fry the onion in a pan with half the oil. When softened, after 4-5 minutes, remove half the onion along with a little of the oil and put into a separate pan. Set aside. Add the garlic and ginger to the original pan and cook for 2 minutes, making sure the garlic does not burn.

Add 250ml of the stock, the zucchini flesh, lemon juice and rind, sweet chilli sauce, sugar, and half the saffron strands (optional). Cook over a medium heat until a thickish sauce has been achieved (about 15 minutes).

Put the set-aside pan with the held-over onion over a medium heat. Stir in the uncooked rice. Stir until the rice is coated with the oil (1-2 minutes). Pour in the remaining stock and saffron (if using). Turn the heat to very low, cover the pan and allow the rice to cook for 15 minutes. Add a little water if the rice starts to dry out.

When the rice is cooked, pan-fry the fish in the remaining olive oil until it is just cooked – 2-3 minutes each side should be enough. Blanch the set-aside zucchini peel strips for 1 minute in boiling water, and drain.

Top the rice with the fish fillets and the sauce. Garnish with the zucchini peel strips and chopped coriander.

Barra Cordon Bleu

A dish created at Club Med, Lindeman Island by chef Marc Monpert, using locally caught fish. Marc served it with noodles, carrot, zucchini and a rich tomato sauce.

Serves 4

INGREDIENTS

4 thick fillets of barramundi or other white fish (approx. 150g each)

8 slices smoked salmon

4 tbsp grated cheese (preferably mild, such as mozzarella)

plain flour, seasoned with salt and pepper

a little oil for frying

1 medium zucchini, peeled and cut into julienne strips

1 large carrot, peeled and cut into julienne strips

200g fettuccine, cooked al dente and drained

Sauce

4 or 5 medium ripe tomatoes, (or 1 x 425g can of peeled tomatoes)

1 tbsp extra virgin olive oil

1 tbsp mild honey

4 or 5 basil leaves

METHOD

Butterfly the fish fillets by cutting them horizontally until almost through to the other side. Open them up, and put a couple of slices of smoked salmon inside. Top with the grated cheese.

Dust the fillets with the seasoned flour, shaking off excess, and pan-fry in a little oil until lightly cooked (about 2 minutes each side).

Blanch the zucchini and carrot strips and plunge the noodles into boiling water to reheat. Drain. Mix the vegetables through the noodles.

To make the sauce: Cook the tomatoes in a hot pan with the oil for 2-3 minutes. Place them in a blender adding the honey and basil leaves. Puree.

Serve the fish on top of the noodles and pour over the tomato, basil and honey sauce.

Finn's Fish

A recipe from Bethany Finn, executive chef at the Hilton Adelaide.

Serves 4

INGREDIENTS
50g shajira spice (see hint)
sea salt
180g salmon fillets
2 cloves garlic, roughly
    chopped
2 tsp chopped ginger
½ onion, finely chopped
1 tsp ground coriander
½ tsp turmeric
flesh of 1 large tomato,
    chopped
½ cup natural yoghurt
200g can of chick peas
2 spinach leaves, roughly cut
vegetable oil

METHOD
Dry roast or toast the shajira spice. Grind with a mortar and pestle or blend in a food processor. Mix with a little sea salt. Sprinkle this mixture on the salmon fillet and allow to stand. Grind the garlic and ginger with a mortar and pestle or in a food processor.

Fry the onion in oil until soft. Add the garlic and ginger paste and fry for 1 minute.

Add the coriander, shajira spice and turmeric. Continue to cook for 1-2 minutes. Add the tomato and yoghurt. Add the canned chick peas and simmer for 15 minutes or so, stirring in the spinach leaves just before serving.

Pan-fry the salmon, a couple of minutes for each side. Serve the salmon on top of the chick pea curry.

Handy hint: Shajira spice is also known as royal cumin and is darker than the common cumin. It is not easy to find, so you can substitute with ground common cumin.

Magnificent Mullet

No matter what anyone may tell you, mullet is a tasty and highly nutritious fish and is rarely treated with the respect it deserves. This dish was served to me by Judith Ham of the Queensland Fish Authority. I believe it is best created on the hot plate of a barbecue. Leaving the scales on helps to keep the fish in shape.

Serves 4

INGREDIENTS

4 mullet, boned and made into butterfly fillets, leaving scales on (ask your fishmonger to do this)

flesh of 2 medium tomatoes, finely chopped

1 spanish onion, finely chopped

1 leek, finely shredded lengthwise

1 tbsp grated parmesan cheese

oil for brushing on mullet

METHOD

Brush the oil on to the scales of the mullet. Turn the fish over (the fish will cook scale side down).

Top each fish with a little of the other ingredients. Put the fish on a barbecue hot plate. Cover the the fillets with aluminium foil.

Allow to cook for 3-4 minutes (depending on the size of the fish and the heat of the plate).

Serving suggestion: Best served with a wedge of polenta and a rocket salad.

Handy hint: The vegetables don't have to cook through, but the fish should be.

Tataki

A dish created by chef Jonathan Alston. Salmon can also be used if you wish.

Serves 4

INGREDIENTS

1 tbsp szechuan pepper
2 tsp rock salt
2 tsp almond meal
1 fillet of tuna or salmon (500g)
2 tsp english mustard
fresh coriander leaves
    (garnish)
lime wedges (garnish)

Cucumber salad

1 english cucumber
few sheets wakame, soaked
    and washed
1 red chilli, sliced (seeds
    removed)
2 tsp toasted sesame seeds
150g cooked noodles
    (Jonathan uses squid ink
    noodles)

Dressing

2 tbsp soy sauce
2 tbsp mirin
½ tsp palm sugar (or other
    sugar)
½ tsp ginger juice (or finely
    chopped ginger)
1 tsp lime juice
½ tsp fish sauce
65ml chicken stock

METHOD

To make the fish: Mix together the pepper, rock salt and almond meal. Sear the fish in a very hot non-stick pan until all the sides are lightly browned. The fish should not be cooked through.

Mix the mustard with a little water to a smooth paste. Lightly coat the fish with the mixture. Roll in the pepper and salt mixture. Slice to serve.

To make the cucumber salad: Mix all the dressing ingredients together. Peel and remove the seeds from the cucumber. Cut it into thin strips. Toss all the salad ingredients in a bowl. Serve the salad on individual plates topped with slices of the fish and cover with the dressing. Garnish with fresh coriander leaves, lime wedges and toasted sesame seeds.

Fish Saffron Citrus Sauce

A recipe from the repertoire of chef Bruce Charlton. It was prepared with Queensland red emperor, but will work with any good white fish fillets. The fish is steamed over a bath of ingredients which then are reduced to make a delicious light sauce, that doesn't mask the delicate flavour of the fish.

METHOD

Drizzle a little oil over fish, season with a little of the orange rind, drizzle over a little orange and lemon juice and sprinkle on a little of the chopped herbs. Leave for an hour or two in the refrigerator to marinate.

Lightly and slowly cook capsicum, onion, 1/4 teaspoon orange rind, saffron strands (or turmeric) and chopped basil in pan with a couple of teaspoons of oil.

When capsicum has softened, add remaining orange and lemon juice and Pernod and reduce again over a low heat for three to four minutes.

Put fish fillets into steamer(s). Steam fish until cooked over the vegetable, herb and fruit juice mixture. Remove fish and keep in warm place while sauce is reduced. Boil sauce to reduce to a creamy consistency.

Serve fish topped with sauce and the capsicum and onion which cooked in the sauce and sprinkle with the remaining herbs.

Note: Pernod is an aniseed liqueur. You could substitute with finely chopped fennel or omit altogether for a less aniseed flavour.

Serves 4

INGREDIENTS

light olive oil
4 white fish fillets (125g each)
1 tsp grated orange rind
300ml orange juice
50ml lemon juice
2 tbsp chopped basil
2 tbsp chopped dill or parsley
flesh of 1/2 red, 1/2 yellow and 1/2 green capsicum, finely chopped
1/2 onion, finely chopped
pinch saffron strands (or turmeric)
1 tbsp Pernod (see note)

Culinary Challenges

By now it was 11:30 and the temperature was in the early forties. A sauce was made on the outdoor stove – we almost didn't need the gas on.

There are few things I like more than a good challenge. I don't mean like bungee jumping (any fool can do that with both feet tied together). And after all, it's gravity that does all the work. Nor do I mean great big challenges like space travel. (Besides, where is gravity then when you need it?)

No, I mean challenges which really count: the food challenges. Like consuming sheep eyes, beef 'pizzles', or rancid yak butter at formal dinners, where refusal may offend. Or cooking in weird circumstances.

During the early days of *Consuming Passions*, I had the gauntlet thrown down to me by a Telstra (then Telecom) staffer named Warren. He wrote: "It's all very well for people with kitchens to cook your recipes, but what about people like me working in the bush? How about doing something for us blokes."

Warren's job was to do the dishes, satellite dishes that is. Most of his working life involved travelling around the country servicing the communications network of remote facilities.

I decided without further ado to take up his challenge. I slip-slop-slapped with the sun screen, donned heavy work boots, tropical shorts, shirt and a solar topi and I set out in the trusty 4WD with a couple of basic utensils, some ingredients, and our TV crew.

On this December day in outback Western Australia it was 35°C by 9 am. We found Warren and set up a portable kitchen, one gas burner, one large pan, and nothing much else.

There was no refrigerator, so red wine was the order of the day. And the dish of the day was to be pasta with a vodka and tomato sauce, one of those simple stand-by dishes which can be prepared from ingredients you can keep in the kitchen for emergencies.

I used penne, large tubular pasta which holds sauces beautifully. This was cooked first, drained and tossed with a little oil. By now it was 11:30 and the temperature was in the early forties. The crew were all under

'There are few things I like more than a challenge...'

umbrellas, whereas Warren and I were forced to remain in the open for the benefit of the director, the camera operator – and eventually the viewer.

A sauce was made by allowing onion and garlic to sweat – they weren't the only ones – in a little extra virgin olive oil.

Then canned tomatoes and tomato paste were added and the liquid was reduced to a smooth, rich sauce over low heat. We almost didn't need the gas on!

While this was happening it allowed me to explain to my guest that it was possible to cook substantial and interesting meals in the most trying conditions and about the foods that made that possible, such as canned fruit and vegetables.

A small amount of chilli went in next, a grating of nutmeg and a splash of vodka.

The drained pasta was stirred through and the dish was almost ready. Just a grating of parmesan cheese to add. Even this ingredient had survived the punishing heat, though it looked a little the worse for wear, more like a block of oily soap. I was not looking much better and by now the flies were winning a battle against the strongest bush-strength insect repellant I could plaster on to myself. I imagined how friendly they would have been if I had been cooking meat or fish. Another of the benefits of vegetarian fare.

Time to serve and Warren's appetite was not affected by the conditions. He even enjoyed a small glass of the Cabernet Sauvignon, which by now was the temperature at which tea is gulpable.

This had been a valuable exercise for me. It made me realise that as Proverbs once said, 'Necessity is the mother of invention'. (These days amended to include the father.) It also made me appreciate what a terrific job these unsung heroes of the workforce do in outback Australia. And I lost about 2kg. I went back to the city and began work compiling a series of recipes which are suitable for those occasions when you hear someone say: "Why don't you all come over to my place and I'll knock up something?" and you realise with some horror that it was you who said it.

The Emergency Kitchen

Here are some of the indispensable ingredients – in addition to the obvious spices – which I make sure I always have on hand:

- Canned fruits, especially apricots, plums and peaches.
- Canned tomatoes, tomato paste, beans and chick peas.
- Canned anchovies or the Fremantle Auschovies (if you can find them).
- Cubes of frozen homemade stock or cartons of stock.
- Lemons and limes.
- Frozen kaffir lime leaves for when I cannot find fresh ones.
- A range of rices and pastas.
- Couscous and polenta.
- Oils, sesame, extra virgin olive, and peanut or canola.
- Balsamic vinegar.
- Hot chilli sauce and Thai sweet chilli sauce.
- A block of parmesan cheese.
- Soya sauces, dark and light reduced salt, tamari.
- Cans of ghee (clarified butter used in Indian cuisine.)
- Dried beans, lentils and peas.
- Honey, maple syrup, raw and soft brown sugar, icing sugar.
- Nuts.
- Mirin.
- Olives, garlic and onions.
- Frozen peas, sardine fillets, and smoked salmon (all Australian, of course).

Salmon Parcels

Although salmon is not a cheap ingredient, you don't need large portions to make a satisfying dish. In this recipe Tasmanian salmon fillets are baked in parcels with lime, ginger, sesame oil and spring onions and served with a delightful sauce.

Serves 4

INGREDIENTS

1 tbsp extra virgin olive oil

4 salmon fillets (125g each)

2 tsp ginger cut into strips (or minced ginger)

2 tsp grated lime peel (or lemon peel)

1 tsp sesame oil

2 tsp lime juice (or lemon juice)

white pepper

1 tbsp spring onions cut into strips

Sauce

2 tbsp lime juice

2 tbsp fish or chicken stock

4 tbsp fortified wine (port, liqueur muscat, Dubonnet)

2 tsp grated lime peel (or lemon)

1 tsp finely chopped ginger

1 tbsp finely chopped spring onion

1 tbsp butter

METHOD

Cut piece of non-stick baking paper into four pieces, 30cm x 30cm. Brush with olive oil.

Place fillet on one side of paper, add sprinkling of ginger, lime peel, sesame oil, lime juice and pepper and a sprinkling of spring onion strips.

Fold paper over fish, seal all round by rolling paper towards the fish on three sides (fourth side is the fold).

Put on baking tray and bake for 10 minutes at 190°C (it could also be steamed).

To make sauce: Put all ingredients except butter into pan over high heat. Boil to reduce liquor by half. Thicken by adding in butter, a few small pieces at a time, stirring constantly over medium heat until a rich emulsion is reached.

To serve: Strain a little sauce onto each plate, put fish and its topping on to the sauce.

Scallop Parcels

Australian scallops and macadamia nuts are combined with basil, garlic and olive oil mixture, wrapped in filo pastry and lovingly baked in the oven. It could just as easily be done with prawn flesh or chicken meat.

Serves 4

INGREDIENTS

500g scallops
100g macadamia nuts, chopped
1 tsp olive oil
2 cloves garlic chopped
1 tbsp chopped basil leaves
1 tbsp low fat yoghurt
filo pastry

METHOD

Wash and cut the scallops into quarters. Let them drain on kitchen paper.

Make a pesto by placing nuts, oil, garlic and basil leaves into a mortar and pound to a smooth paste. A food processor could be used for this.

Mix in the scallops with the pesto and moisten with a little of the yoghurt.

Spread a few sheets of pastry out on a tea towel. Brush with a little extra light olive oil, folding each sheet onto the one beneath it. Then cut into six squares, put a dollop of scallop mix on each sheet and twist up into parcels. These may be tied with strips of chives or spring onions.

Place on a lightly oiled tray and into a 180°C oven until brown – about 20 minutes.

Seared Tuna with Basil Oil

One of Australia's new breed of chefs is Danny Angove of VAT 107 at Margaret River. Danny combines his skills with top Australian produce.

Serves 4

INGREDIENTS

olive oil for frying

4 x 200g tuna steaks

16 young rocket leaves

3 tbsp balsamic vinegar

4 lime wedges

8 sprigs coriander

cracked pepper

Salsa

1 medium spanish onion, finely diced

1 lebanese cucumber, seeds removed and finely diced

1 red capsicum, finely diced

1 tbsp olive oil

lime juice, to taste

Basil oil

bunch basil, washed and dried

juice of 1 lime

185ml olive oil

cracked black pepper

METHOD

Salsa: Combine all ingredients with a little lime juice, cover and refrigerate.

Basil oil: Place basil in mortar or blender with lime juice and puree. Add olive oil slowly and blend until smooth.

Tuna: Brush a heavy-based frying pan with olive oil and heat until it is smoking. Sear tuna 30-40 seconds each side. Remove and keep warm.

To serve: Cut each tuna steak in half, put on mound of rocket leaves, top with salsa, and drizzle each serving with balsamic vinegar and a little basil oil before garnishing with lime and coriander. Season to taste.

Cobbler Ceviche

A recipe by agricultural research scientist John Bonnardeau. Prepared for Consuming Passions *in Kununurra, where fish is plentiful, as are tropical fruits and the asparagus with which John accompanies the ceviche. John uses the local silver cobbler, a member of the catfish family, but any fish fillets could be used. A pickled dish, Peruvian Cobbler Ceviche a la Peruana, may be made well ahead of eating.*

Serves 4

METHOD

Put fish into a non-reactive dish and pour over lime juice to cover. Top with onion rings and crushed garlic. Sprinkle with sea salt and drizzle over olive oil. Sprinkle with coriander leaves. Cover dish with plastic wrap and refrigerate for at least 12 hours.

For vinaigrette: Trim bottoms of asparagus spears. Blanch asparagus in lightly salted boiling water for 1 minute. Plunge into cold water – the colder the better – to refresh. Drain.

Put olive oil, vinegar and salt and pepper into a screwtop jar and shake well. Pour vinaigrette over asparagus, cover with plastic wrap and refrigerate for 12 hours.

To serve: Arrange fish and asparagus vinaigrette on serving plates.

Leftover potential: Keeps for a couple of days in the refrigerator, but the flesh of the fish may break down.

INGREDIENTS

400g fish fillets, cut into
  2cm strips
200ml lime (or orange or
  lemon) juice
1 spanish (red) onion, very
  thinly sliced
2 cloves garlic, crushed
1 tsp sea salt
1 tbsp extra virgin olive oil
1 tbsp chopped coriander
  leaves

Asparagus Vinaigrette
500g asparagus spears
2 tbsp extra virgin olive oil
2 tsp balsamic vinegar
salt and pepper to taste

Crepes Mentelle

I was inspired to cook this by David Hohnen of Cape Mentelle Wines. I use several seafoods, but it could be made with just one or two.

Serves 6

INGREDIENTS

Pancakes

100g plain flour

100g self-raising flour

2 large eggs

300ml milk

300ml water

1 tsp finely grated lemon rind

pinch salt

light oil or butter for cooking

Filling

400g white fish fillets

200g scallop meat

200g shelled prawns

2 cloves garlic, finely chopped

¼ cup extra virgin olive oil

plain flour

Sauce

1 tbsp butter

1 tbsp plain flour

2 tbsp white wine

250ml chicken or fish stock

250ml milk

¼ tsp ground mace

1 tbsp chopped parsley

salt and pepper to taste

1 tbsp grated parmesan
   cheese to serve

METHOD

Make the pancakes: Mix the two flours with the eggs, then slowly add the milk and water. Add lemon rind and salt and whisk to make a batter with the consistency of pouring cream. Stand for 30 minutes. In a small frying pan (preferably non-stick), heat a little oil or melt a little butter and cook the pancakes. They need not be huge playing field-sized pancakes – 15cm across is about right.

Prepare the seafood: Dry the fish on paper towels and cut into 2.5cm cubes. Dry the scallops on paper towels. Cut the prawns down the back and remove digestive tract, then pat dry on paper towels. Gently cook garlic in olive oil for 2 minutes. Remove garlic and reserve if you wish – this can be added to the sauce later in the recipe.

Toss all the seafood in plain flour, than shake in a sieve to remove surplus flour. Add seafood to the pan and fry as follows – fish for 3 minutes, prawns for 2 minutes and scallops for 1 minute. After each lot of seafood is cooked, remove it from the pan and drain on paper towels. Set aside and keep warm.

Make the sauce: In heavy-based saucepan, melt butter, then stir in flour and cook gently for 2-3 minutes. Stir in wine, a little at a time, and cook, stirring constantly. As the mixture starts to thicken, add stock a little at a time. Once all the wine and stock have been added, stir in milk, a little at a time, and cook until you have a smooth sauce. Stir all the seafood, the reserved garlic (if you like your seafood really garlicky), the mace, parsley and salt and pepper into the sauce.

Test a piece of seafood to make sure it's cooked. If it needs any further cooking, let it simmer in the sauce over low heat, otherwise, just keep the mixture warm.

Assemble: Put a couple of pancakes on each dinner plate. Put a generous amount of seafood on one side of each pancake, fold pancake over seafood filling, sprinkle with cheese. Serve as is or put under a preheated hot grill and brown briefly.

Moroccan Fish

One of the principal mixtures which gives a distinctive flavour to Moroccan savoury cooking is chermoula, a blend of spices, herbs, onion, lemon juice and oil. It works well for both fish and meats. The quantities of spices given are suitable for most purposes, but can be adjusted to suit your taste after you've tried it.

Serves 4

INGREDIENTS

1 tsp ground coriander
$1/2$ tsp ground cinnamon
1 tsp ground cumin
1 tsp ground paprika
1 tsp ground ginger
1 small onion, finely chopped
4 cloves garlic, finely chopped
1 tbsp finely chopped parsley
   (preferably flat-leaf)
1 tbsp finely chopped fresh
   coriander
1 small chilli, seeds removed,
   finely chopped (or you
   could use chilli sauce)
a few strands of saffron
   (optional)
2 tbsp lemon juice
3 tbsp nut oil, such as
   macadamia oil (or other oil
   of your choice can be used)
4 fish fillets or cutlets

METHOD

Make a chermoula by mixing together the spices in a bowl – grinding them if they are not powdery. Add all remaining ingredients except oil and fish.

Slowly dribble in oil, a little at a time, stirring constantly (as if making mayonnaise). Continue adding oil until all has been incorporated.

Rub fish with the chermoula and marinate for at least 1 hour. Pan-fry fish, preferably in a non-stick pan. Even in other frying pans the oil in the chermoula should be enough to prevent the fish from sticking.

Serving suggestion: I like to serve this dish with couscous made up according to instructions on the packet.

Leftover potential: Chermoula keeps for several days in the refrigerator.

"I have known many
meat eaters to be far more
non-violent than vegetarians."

MAHATMA GANDHI

Meat

Beef and Juniper Hotpot

This dish was created to celebrate and accompany the Cape Mentelle Shiraz 1994. Beef pieces are marinated in Shiraz along with juniper berries, bay leaves and a little olive oil, then simmered to voluptuous perfection with potatoes, carrots, garlic, stock and prunes.

Serves 4

INGREDIENTS

750g chuck steak, cut into
   cubes
250ml Cape Mentelle Shiraz
8 or 9 juniper berries, crushed
2 dried bay leaves
2 tbsp olive oil
seasoned flour for
   dusting meat
1 tbsp butter
1 large onion, quartered
2 medium carrots, sliced
4 cloves garlic
750ml chicken or veal stock
8 pitted prunes, quartered
salt and pepper to taste
1 tbsp finely chopped parsley

METHOD

In a large bowl, combine meat, wine, juniper berries, bay leaves and I tablespoon olive oil. Marinate for 2 hours at room temperature or overnight in the refrigerator.

Drain and reserve marinating liquid. Dry meat on paper towels and toss in seasoned flour. Put meat in a sieve and shake off surplus flour (this is important if you don't want a beef cake!)

In a large, deep frying pan or stock pot, brown meat cubes a few at a time, over medium heat, in a mixture of the olive oil and butter. Remove from pan.

Sauté onion, carrots and garlic in same pan for 4-5 minutes. Remove and place with meat.

Deglaze pan with stock and reserved wine mixture and cook for 2 minutes.

Return meat and vegetables to pan. Add prunes, cover tightly and simmer gently for 2 hours or until meat is tender. Just before serving, season to taste and stir in the parsley.

Serving suggestion: Serve with creamy mashed potatoes.

Leftover potential: Keeps for a couple of days in the refrigerator. Reheat over low heat before serving.

Kangaroo and Spicy Lentils

Kangaroo and Spicy Lentils

Serves 4

INGREDIENTS

1 tbsp extra virgin olive oil
4 pieces kangaroo fillet (about 150g each)

Lentils

1 small onion, finely chopped
1 small carrot, chopped into small dice
3 cloves garlic, chopped
2 tbsp olive oil
1 tspn ground ginger
1 tbsp ground cumin
1/2 tspn cardamom seeds
1/2 cup brown of green lentils
2 cups chicken stock
1 cup mixture of chopped basil, mint and coriander

METHOD

For the lentils, simmer onion, carrot and garlic in a little olive oil for 3 minutes. Add ginger, cumin and cardamom and cook for 2 minutes. Add lentils and stock and simmer for 1 hour or until mixture reduces to a thickish consistency. Stir in herbs.

Shortly before serving, brush kangaroo with oil and sear in a very hot pan for 2-3 minutes – the meat should be cooked rare to medium-rare. Rest meat for a few minutes before serving. Serve kangaroo with the spicy lentils.

Serving suggestion: Just add a tossed green salad to make a complete meal.

Leftover potential: Best eaten immediately after cooking.

Hint: Though kangaroo fillets are used for this dish, you could substitute lean fillet steak.

Lamb Harissa

Northern Africa is the source of this highly seasoned dish. Try seasoning vegetables, fish and poultry with the harissa.

Serves 6

INGREDIENTS

1 tbsp chopped fresh mint
1 tbsp chopped fresh oregano
   (or coriander)
50g lean lamb (fillet or
   backstrap), cut into large
   pieces
300ml chicken stock

Harissa

50g dried chillies, split and
   seeds removed (or 2 or 3
   tsp minced chilli)
1 tsp coriander seeds
2 tsp caraway seeds
1 tsp cumin seeds
3 or 4 cloves garlic
4 tbsp oil (olive, canola,
   macadamia)

METHOD

To make harissa: Soak chilli flesh in hot water. Meanwhile, grind together coriander, caraway and cumin in a mortar or food processor. Ready ground spices can be used, but it's not quite the same. Add garlic and grind until the garlic breaks down. Drain the chillies, chop, add to the spice mixture and continue to grind. Slowly add oil a few drops at a time. This is the basic harissa.

For this dish, spoon 2 tablespoons of harissa (or more if you like your food really hot) into a bowl, stir in mint and oregano. Add lamb and toss to coat. Set aside to marinate or you can cook the lamb immediately.

About 20 minutes before you are ready to serve, quickly pan-fry (preferably in a non-stick pan) the lamb for 3-4 minutes on each side – take care not to overcook it. Remove lamb from pan, cover and keep warm.

Deglaze pan with stock over medium heat, then cook to reduce to a sauce with a thick consistency. Serve spooned over lamb.

Serving suggestion: Serve lamb with a currant and pine nut pilau. I'd recommend a pinot noir to accompany this dish. Australian, of course.

Leftover potential: Keeps for 1 or 2 days in the refrigerator. The basic harissa keeps well in the refrigerator.

Manchamantel Pork

South-west American cuisine has yet to make its mark in Australia, but it will one day. This dish combines pineapple, banana and apple in a sauce to accompany pork. It is a clean as well as a lean dish, as are many from this part of the world. The recipe, like many from New Mexico, relies on chillies that have flavour rather than heat. Such chillies are becoming available. In their absence you could use a small amount of chilli sauce, but it won't be quite the same.

Serves 4

INGREDIENTS

2 medium tomatoes

1 cup banana pieces

1 cup chopped pineapple pieces

1 cup peeled apple pieces

2 dried ancho chillies (see hint) or 1 tsp chilli sauce

$1/4$ tsp allspice

$1/4$ tsp ground cinnamon

$1/2$ tsp white pepper

1 tbsp rice vinegar

4 pork chops

1 tsp sesame oil

3 tsp tamari soya sauce

METHOD

Roast tomatoes over a flame until the skins blacken (this is an important contributor to the dish's flavour).

Puree tomatoes, banana, pineapple, apple and chillies in a food processor (or add chilli sauce at this time if using). Add spices and vinegar and puree to combine. The mixture should be quite liquid. If it is not, add a little water.

Strain mixture, then put into a frying pan with a little oil and cook for 5 minutes to consolidate the flavours and reduce the mixture to a thick sauce.

Sear pork chops in sesame oil and soya sauce in a frying pan. Transfer to an ovenproof dish and bake at 190°C for about 15 minutes. Alternatively, continue cooking in the frying pan. Serve with a generous quantity of the fruity Manchamantel sauce.

Leftover potential: Best eaten immediately.

Hint: If using large Mexican chillies, remove stalk and seeds and lightly roast chillies in a dry pan, then simmer in a large quantity of near-boiling water for 20 minutes.

Irish, no question!

It was nearly 1 am when the local policeman – the garda – finally threw them, and me, out. "This hasn't happened in six years," said the publican.

my intention was to write a chapter of the moral history of my country and I chose Dublin for the scene because that city seemed to me the centre of paralysis' – this is what James Joyce wrote in a letter in 1905.

One of the most extraordinary telephone calls I have ever received was in the wee small hours of a winter morning during the height of the British beef scare. "David Zebedee here," said the strongly-flavoured, sing-song Irish voice. "And I have a problem."

It transpired that this gentleman – one of whose more obvious problems was that he had no idea of the time difference between Dublin, Ireland, and Perth, Australia – needed to find an alternative to the beef-based hamburgers he had been selling at his AbraKebabra chain of eateries.

"I saw your recipe for the Aussie Lamburger in Consuming Passions on the telly here and wondered if I could use your recipe in my outlets," he enthused.

Stunned and flattered, I faxed it off to him.

This was my introduction to the Irish hospitality industry, of which I'm now convinced there's no equal.

Hospitality is synonymous with Ireland. From the moment you touch down at Dublin airport you can't help feeling at home, an unusual experience in a capital city, and this is the capital of the Irish Republic, the fastest growing economy in Europe. For this gastronaut it was the starting point for an extraordinary sensual journey.

First stop was the Shelbourne Hotel on lovely St Stephen's Green. This is one of those charming old-fashioned hotels which has escaped 'progress'. Highly ornate ceilings, large open fires, vintage landscapes on the wall, porters in heavy woollen jackets and waistcoats , the sweet-sounding Irish lilt everywhere and a gently wafting aroma of fine cigars. Massive drapes and fresh flowers are everywhere, and waitresses primly dressed in black and white weave their way through tables with trays of silver service afternoon teas. Tradition kept alive.

This is where in days gone by you might have bumped into W. B. Yeats, Thackeray or James Joyce himself, and it still rings with the romance of bygone days. Built in 1842, this grande dame of hotels ranks with Melbourne's Hotel Windsor as one of those institutions which deserves to be preserved at all cost.

The only old-fashioned thing about the food served in its 27 On The Green restaurant was the quality. I launched into an excursion through five items on the menu: Irish smoked salmon, scallops, quail, ravioli of wild mushrooms, and a millefeuille of pears.

Breakfast in Dublin must be taken at a Bewleys. There are several of these exceptional cafés, but the one that's a must is in Grafton Street. Again an historic establishment – opened in 1840 – it appears to have changed very little in appearance: wood panelling, stained-glass, large eating areas, and traditionally dressed staff. The difference is that it's now self-service, with a range of sensible options such as fresh fruit, yoghurts, cereals, and breads, plus the more heavy going delights of sausages, eggs, baked beans and the ubiquitous black pudding, the heavy duty sausage that is seen throughout the Emerald Isle. And the coffee is – to use an expression favoured by TV character Blackadder, 'as thick as a whale omelette.' A real kick start to the day.

A walk through St Stephen's Green and Trinity College – where the legendary Book of Kells is displayed – past the Clarence Hotel (owned by members of the band U2) and into Temple Bar, takes one to the Winding Stair Bookshop. It's not often you enter a bookshop and are confronted with the smell of soup, but it happens here, rich thick lentil soup with bacon hocks. A leisurely browse to the accompaniment of cool jazz is just the thing to take one on to the delights of lunch.

Fine food is everywhere in Dublin, with quality produce available at places with such whimsical names as Ow Valley Farm Shop, Blazing Salads II, and Ta Sé Mohogani Gaspipes – this one in the suburb of Stoneybatter!

La Stampa won my vote for Ireland's best dining room, and had some pretty fine food to match. It was like stepping into Dr Who's Tardis. The unassuming entrance, narrow bar and reception area opened into a large,

An episode of *Consuming Passions* brought an unexpected phone call from Ireland one morning.

Ian with his own wine, Artamus.

Dublin has an energy, a timelessness and a generosity of spirit that makes this city one of the world's greatest. Certainly, there is no sign of paralysis.

Down South...

My first stop after Dublin was Ballymaloe. Just say the name to food professionals around the world and they will say "Darina Allen". It was she who made the Ballymaloe Cookery School famous through her television cooking shows and books, but it was her mother-in-law Myrtle who was at the vanguard of the Irish culinary revolution.

On the south coast in Cork, Ballymaloe House became one of the country's leading restaurants in the 1960s, when Mrs Allen, a farmer's wife living on a 400-acre farm, decided to open part of the house as a restaurant. She never looked back.

Now Ballymalloe House is one of the world's finest country houses, offering accommodation with very fine fare.

The school is one of the world's best, catering for up to 44 students at a time, and not just for cooking classes. There are also courses on Ireland's food culture and tradition, on foraging for mushrooms and other wild foods, on gardening, even on shell decoration.

The emphasis at Ballymaloe is on fine local produce, and that extends to superb cheeses, eggs that taste as newly laid as they are, and herbs from the parterre gardens.

The home-grown produce crops up in such dishes as blackcurrant leaf sorbet, crab croquettes, turkey baked with Meursault wine and morels, served with buttered Spring cabbage, and Ballycotton fish soup which is chock full of seafood brought into the nearby fishing village of that name.

It was at this picturesque fishing harbour that I did my first blind tasting of Irish stout at one of the many pubs named after local

cathedral-like restaurant with huge mirrors, candles in fancy candlesticks, candelabra, glassed screens, statues and palms. Music ranged from French accordion pieces to laid-back jazz to the theme from Twin Peaks. Spotlights shone down on dried flower arrangements, waiters wafted around wearing hand painted waistcoats.

Their breast of duck roasted with local honey and thyme and served with braised witloof and spring onions, and their confit of guinea fowl with buttered cabbage and a Calvados jus with a hint of caraway, transported me to palate paradise.

There are dozens of great restaurants, cafés and pubs, and scores of quality food shops making this gateway to Ireland a foodie haven.

identities, in this case potter Stephen Pearce.

A firm devotee of Guinness, I already knew the outcome – or so I thought.

A small, vocal crowd gathered in the tiny bar as several large glasses of the black foaming brew were placed before me. I sniffed, sipped, slurped and let the creaming stouts wash round my palate. I went through them again, then I made my selection of the first three. "You're sure?" asked Stephen Pearce, when I had told him which ones I preferred. "Absolutely," I replied. Then he announced what I'd chosen: "First, Murphy's. Second, Beamish. Third Guinness." Guinness came third? What a sobering experience, but then in Cork as anywhere else, I suppose, life is full of surprises and of course I should have known that the local brew would turn out to be best.

Another surprise was in store for me at the Cork fishing village of Baltimore, where I found a splendid restaurant run by a brace of Australians, chef Susan Holland and her partner Ian Parr.

At the Customs House, these former Sydneysiders made the most of the catch of the day: Squid served with a preserved-lemon salsa, turbot fillets with a light beurre blanc and fresh young beans, hake grilled and served atop olive oil mashed potato.

Whether it's the local goat cheeses or the smoked salmon, the Irish share Australia's concern that quality is not compromised in the food industry. At all their restaurants and hotels I visited, the traditional soda bread or a molasses bread were offered, freshly made each morning on the premises. Just one of those small touches that help make Ireland the inviting country it is.

One highlight of my tour was a visit to the Hairy Spaniard pub in Kinsale, a pretty fishing town about 30km south of Cork city with quite a gastronomic history. For a town of some 2,500 souls, there's an amazing number of eating and drinking houses in the area. At the Hairy Spaniard, as you so often find in Ireland, the entertainment is as free flowing as the tipple. A doctor, a mathematician, a chef and a professional musician played acoustic traditional jigs and reels to a packed house. It was nearly 1 am when the local policeman – the garda – finally threw them, and me, out. "This hasn't happened in six years," said the apologetic publican. "And on a Wednesday night, too!"

Before visiting Ireland I had been told – by several Irish ex-pats (forgive the pun) – not to plan the trip, beyond booking the first night. Just go with the flow seemed to be the way to go. And so it proved.

Ireland must be enjoyed like a fine old wine, slowly and with wonder.

And it's a guarantee that once visited, you'll be going back for more. I will. I haven't yet experienced AbraKebabra.

If the soup had been as warm as the claret...
If the claret had been as old as the chicken...
If the chicken had been as fat as our host...
It would have been a splendid meal.

DONALD McCULLOUGH *After Dinner Grace* 1960

Moussaka

A Consuming Passions version of this Greek – or it could be Turkish – classic. It's a much lighter dish than the moussaka that's customarily served in restaurants.

Serves 4

INGREDIENTS

1 large eggplant, cut into 1cm thick slices

salt

olive oil

500g minced lamb (or you could use beef)

2 tbsp finely chopped onion

200ml red wine

1 tsp allspice

1 large can tomatoes (about 800g)

1 tbsp chicken or veal stock

1 tsp chilli sauce

4 cloves garlic, crushed

2 tsp chopped rosemary (or ½ tsp dried)

1 tbsp butter

3 tbsp cornflour

500ml reduced fat milk

100g low fat mozzarella cheese, grated

1 tbsp parmesan cheese, grated

½ tsp grated nutmeg

pepper to taste

METHOD

Sprinkle eggplant with salt and stand for 30 minutes to remove bitter juices. Wash, drain and dry on paper towels. Brush eggplant with olive oil. Put on baking trays and bake at 180°C for 20 minutes, or until softened. This technique means that less oil is absorbed than if using the more traditional method of frying the eggplant.

Cook meat in a little olive oil until it changes colour. It doesn't need to be thoroughly cooked at this stage.

Add onion, wine, allspice, tomatoes, stock, chilli sauce, garlic and rosemary. Crush the tomatoes and cook slowly until mixture reduces to a thick sauce – about 40 minutes.

Make a roux by melting the butter over medium heat, stir in cornflour and cook for 2-3 minutes – but don't allow it to brown. Slowly stir in milk and simmer, stirring, until you have a smooth sauce.

Stir in mozzarella and parmesan cheeses and nutmeg. Season to taste.

To assemble: Alternate layers of eggplant with the tomato sauce in a baking dish, starting with a little sauce. Finally top with the bechamel sauce. Bake at 190°C for 30-40 minutes or until top is nicely browned.

Leftover potential: Good.

Hint: Can be made in advance, up to the cooking stage, and refrigerated. Allow 15 minutes longer cooking time if it's going straight from the refrigerator to the oven.

Spicy Spare Ribs

Pork spare ribs are marinated in a mixture of honey, five spice, coriander, sherry, sesame oil, soya sauce, chilli and bottled tomato sauce. Although the half-kilo per person I allow may seem like a lot, remember that much of the weight is bone. This heavenly concoction is best made the day before it's cooked to allow the ribs to acquire the spiciness which makes the dish such a success.

Serves 4

METHOD

Marinade: Mix together all marinade ingredients (omit chilli if serving to small children who may not care for it). Toss ribs in the marinade, put in an airtight container and refrigerate for at least 4 hours, or preferably overnight. Before cooking, drain ribs well and reserve marinade.

Sear ribs, a few at a time, in oil in a wok or frying pan to brown, then transfer to a baking tray.

Bake the ribs at 210°C for 25 minutes (or until cooked), or they may also be barbecued. Whichever way you choose to cook them, baste frequently with the marinade.

To serve, toss with the coriander leaves and spring onions and eat with your fingers.

Leftover potential: No, eat immediately.

Hint: When buying spare ribs, make sure there is meat on the bones. Tell the butcher how you intend using the ribs and I'm sure he – or she – will oblige. Ask for them to be cut into individual ribs. My preference is for pork ribs, but you could use beef.

INGREDIENTS

2 kg pork spare ribs (or beef, see hint)
2 tbsp oil
2 tbsp chopped coriander leaves to serve
2 tbsp chopped spring onions to serve

Marinade
2 tbsp sherry
2 tbsp honey
2 tbsp light soya sauce
2 tsp sesame oil
300ml tomato sauce
½ tsp five spice powder
1 tsp ground coriander seeds
1 tsp minced chilli or to taste

Rapid Roast Pork

Roasting is one of the oldest methods of cooking meat and was done on open fires long before ovens were invented. One of the challenges today is to roast the meat cuts, which are now leaner than they used to be, without drying them out. One of the quickest and easiest roasts is this one, which cooks in about 20 minutes.

Serves 2

INGREDIENTS

1 tbsp reduced salt soya
     sauce
1 tsp sesame oil
1 pork fillet (about 250g)
1 large apple, sliced
3 crushed juniper berries
sprig fresh thyme
2 tsp honey
2 rashers lean bacon

METHOD

Combine soya sauce and sesame oil and smear over pork. Sear pork in a very hot frying pan (preferably non-stick), for 30 seconds each side.

Lightly oil a baking tray, arrange apple slices in a single row to form a bed for the pork. Scatter with juniper berries and thyme.

Warm honey and brush over pork. Put pork on apples, cover with bacon and roast at 200°C for 15 minutes. Stand in warm place for 5 minutes to rest before carving.

Serving suggestion: Cut pork into medallions and serve with apple from under the fillet and apple chutney.

Leftover potential: This roast is delicious cold, but is best eaten the same day.

Veal Casserole

Veal shank, or shin, is perfect in slowly cooked casseroles, where the texture of the meat remains and the bones and marrow provide a bliss factor. Ask your butcher to bone the shin and give you the meat and bones.

Serves 4

INGREDIENTS

1 large boned veal shank and
   the bones
1 tbsp olive oil
1 large onion, cut into large
   pieces
1 or 2 medium carrots,
   chopped
1 parsnip, peeled and
   chopped
2 slender young leeks, sliced
300ml white wine
   (chardonnay is fine)
2 tbsp tomato paste
4 or 5 sprigs thyme
4 or 5 sprigs parsley
1 or 2 bay leaves
3 or 4 prunes, pitted and
   finely chopped
3 or 4 cloves garlic, peeled
   and cut into thin strips
1 x 375g can kidney beans,
   drained
2 cups cooked ribbon pasta,
   such as fettuccine

METHOD

Make a stock by placing the veal bones in a stockpot or large saucepan, cover with water and simmer for 4-5 hours. Skim top as necessary. Drain and remove fat. Cook stock over medium heat until reduced by half. Rather than making your own veal stock, chicken stock can be used instead – if using chicken stock omit this step.

Cut veal meat into 4cm cubes and sauté in olive oil until just brown. Drain and place into a casserole dish.

Sauté onion, carrots, parsnip and leeks in remaining oil for 2-3 minutes. Remove and put into casserole.

Deglaze pan with wine, then stir in tomato paste and 500ml of veal stock. Pour wine mixture into casserole and add thyme, parsley, bay leaves and prunes. Cover and bake at 160°C for at least 2 hours or until meat is very tender.

Put garlic on a small baking tray and dry in oven for a few minutes. Set aside.

When casserole is cooked, stir in beans and pasta and heat for a few minutes longer. Serve topped with dried garlic chips and garnished with fresh parsley and thyme.

Leftover potential: Keeps for 2 or 3 days in the refrigerator.

Herb Crusted Lamb with Rosemary Potatoes

A beautiful way to serve lamb – roasted and dished-up with baked herbed potatoes.

Serves 6

INGREDIENTS

750g new potatoes or old
   potatoes, quartered
3 tbsp finely chopped
   rosemary leaves
extra virgin olive oil
10 cloves garlic
6 sage leaves, finely chopped
6 sprigs thyme, finely
   chopped
2 tbsp finely chopped parsley
6 racks of lamb, each
   containing 4 cutlets, (well-
   trimmed by the butcher)
4 tbsp grainy mild mustard

METHOD

Toss the potatoes with 2 tablespoons of rosemary and a little olive oil and put in a baking tray. Bake at 210°C for 30 minutes (before starting to cook the lamb).

Puree the garlic with a couple of teaspoons of olive oil. Mix 1 tablespoon of rosemary with the sage, thyme and parsley. Spread the garlic puree over the racks of lamb. Cover with a thin layer of grainy mustard. Sprinkle with the herb mixture and pat down.

In a pan, sear the crusted meat in hot olive oil for a couple of minutes. Place on a baking tray, crust side up and bake for 30 minutes (leaving the potatoes in to continue cooking). Allow the lamb to stand in warm place for 5 or 10 minutes before serving.

Hint: Depending on the size of the lamb racks, you may need to cook longer, if you like your meat well done.

Serving suggestion: Serve with the potatoes, mixed salad greens or spinach, and a reduction of the pan juice or stock.

Wine choice: A young shiraz is perfect with lamb.

Massaman Curry of Beef

*An adaptation of a
Muslim classic.
Although I have used
beef here, other meats
may be substituted.*

Serves 4

INGREDIENTS
750g lean beef, cut into
    small cubes
oil for frying
500g potatoes, washed and
    cut into small cubes
2 tsp tamarind paste
    (optional)
150ml coconut milk
2 bay leaves

Curry paste
1 tsp peppercorns
2 tsp coriander seeds
seeds from 6 cardamom pods
2 tsp cumin seeds
3 or 4 cloves
6 or 7 cloves garlic
4 or 5 shallots
1 tbsp dried shrimps (or 2 tsp
    shrimp paste) (optional)
1 tsp chopped peeled lemon
    grass stalk (optional)
1 tsp grated lime or lemon rind

METHOD
To make the curry paste: Mix together the peppercorns, coriander seeds, cardamom, cumin, and cloves and toast in a dry frying pan over medium heat for 2-3 minutes, making sure they do not burn.

In a mortar or blender, grind the toasted spices along with the remaining paste ingredients.

Brown the beef in a little oil, remove from the pan. Brown the potatoes in a little oil. Remove from the pan.

Gently fry the curry paste in a little oil, stirring constantly. If using, dissolve the tamarind paste in a little water and strain on top of the curry paste. Bring this mixture to the boil and allow to reduce a little. Stir in the coconut milk.

Add the beef, potatoes and bay leaves and allow to simmer gently until the beef is cooked. Depending on the size of the cubes, this could take an hour or so. Don't cover the pan as the mixture may curdle. Stir occasionally, making sure you don't break up the potatoes towards end of the cooking time.

Serve with vast quantities of steamed or boiled rice.

Sausage Sensation

A dish prepared in honour of Scott and Louisa Wise, the musicians who have provided the music for Consuming Passions. Sausages are baked with caramelised onions, kidney beans, apple and potatoes.

Serves 6

INGREDIENTS

3 or 4 spanish onions (or other), cut into thick slices

1 tbsp extra virgin olive oil

1 tbsp balsamic vinegar

1 tsp sugar

4 sprigs of fresh rosemary (or 1 tsp dried)

10 or 12 pork sausages (such as cumberlands)

2 tsp cornflour

500ml veal or chicken stock

2 medium sized apples, peeled, cored, thinly sliced and tossed with lemon juice to prevent browning

1 can kidney beans (400g or 420g), drained

1 or 2 potatoes peeled and very thinly sliced (with a potato peeler)

METHOD

Put the onion slices on an oiled baking tray. Sprinkle with olive oil, balsamic vinegar, sugar and dried rosemary (if using). Arrange fresh rosemary across the top (if using). Put in an oven at 180°C and allow to brown and caramelise (50 minutes to one hour).

Brown the sausages. Put on a rack over a baking tray and cook in the oven.

Slowly add the cornflour to the stock to thicken and then cook for two or three minutes.

To assemble the casserole, remove the rosemary twigs from the onions. Put the onions in the bottom of an oven-proof dish. Add the sausages and the sliced apple. Add half the beans, pour in half the thickened stock, packing ingredients tightly together.

Add more beans and more thickened stock. Finally, top with the potato slices.

Cover in an oven at 180°C for about 50 minutes. Uncover the dish about 10 minutes before removing.

Lamb Tagine

The tagine is a North African dish, usually of meat cooked with spices and sweetened with fruits or honey.

Serves 4

INGREDIENTS

500g lean lamb (boned leg)
2 tbsp olive oil
1 onion, sliced
juice of one lemon
1 tbsp honey
2 tbsp chopped coriander
    leaves
1 tsp ground coriander
1 tbsp chopped parsley
1 tsp powdered cinnamon
1 tsp powdered cumin
few strands saffron (optional)
1 cup veal or chicken stock
1 cup chopped carrots
1 cup chopped leek
50g almonds lightly browned
    in dry pan or oven browned
couscous or rice to serve
natural yoghurt, pepper,
    paprika and almonds to
    garnish

METHOD

Cut the meat into bite-sized cubes. In large pan, brown it in one tablespoon of olive oil over high heat (about 3 minutes). It is important the pan is hot enough for the lamb to brown without rendering juices and starting to stew. Remove from pan, drain and put in casserole dish.

In the same pan used for browning lamb, put remaining oil, reduce heat and cook onion until softened.

Add the juice of lemon, honey, coriander, parsley and cinnamon, cumin, saffron and stock. Stir well, then add carrots and leek pieces and pour mixture over lamb.

Cover tightly and simmer for 2 hours in very low oven (120°C). A few minutes before cooking time, stir in almonds.

Serve with couscous or rice, garnish with yoghurt, black pepper, paprika and almonds.

Souvlakia

A celebrated Greek dish most of us are familiar with in take-away form.

Serves 6

INGREDIENTS

1.25 kg lean boned lamb, cut
   into 2cm cubes
2 tbsp chopped fresh mint for
   garnish

Marinade
1/2 cup olive oil
1/2 cup dry white wine
juice and finely grated rind of
   1 lemon
3 cloves garlic, crushed
freshly ground black pepper
1 tbsp chopped fresh oregano
   (or 1 tsp dried)
1 onion, grated

METHOD
To make the marinade: Place all ingredients in a non-reactive bowl and mix to combine. Add meat and marinate in the refrigerator for 12-24 hours.

Drain meat and reserve marinade. Thread meat on to skewers and cook on a preheated hot barbecue or under a hot grill, brushing occasionally with marinade until lamb is cooked.

Serve garnished with mint.

Serving suggestion: Delicious served with steamed or boiled rice and a tomato salad.

Souvlakia

Herbed Lamb Balls

Herbed Lamb Balls

Greek-style meat balls made with herbs, spices and just a little parmesan cheese.

Serves 6

INGREDIENTS

500g minced lean lamb
2 tbsp finely chopped onion
2 eggs
1 tbsp finely chopped fresh
   oregano
2 tsp finely chopped fresh
   rosemary
1 tbsp grated parmesan
   cheese
2 tsp ground cumin
½ tsp white pepper
breadcrumbs (preferably
   made from day-old bread)
seasoned flour to coat balls
oil for frying

METHOD
Mix together all ingredients, except the breadcrumbs, flour and
oil. Slowly mix in the breadcrumbs until you have a firm mixture.
You'll probably need about 2 tablespoons of breadcrumbs.

Shape mixture in balls about 3cm in diameter and roll in
seasoned flour.

Either deep-fry or shallow-fry lamb balls in oil for 4-5 minutes.
To check cooking time, try one once it's brown all over.

Serving suggestion: Delicious on their own as a snack or served
with Lemony Mixed Vegetables (page 69).

Leftover potential: Keeps for up to two days in the refrigerator.

Sang Choy Bow

One of my favourite dishes from Hong Kong, this is often referred to as the Chinese hamburger. It's a mixture of pork, mushrooms, onion, bamboo shoots and water chestnuts stir-fried with seasonings and served in a lettuce leaf.

Serves 4

INGREDIENTS

2 tbsp oil

50g onions, finely chopped

1 tsp finely chopped garlic

1 tsp finely chopped ginger

1 tbsp reduced salt soya sauce

few drops sesame oil

250g lean pork (loin, leg steak or schnitzel) minced or finely chopped

50g button mushrooms, finely chopped

50g water chestnuts, finely chopped

50g bamboo shoots, finely chopped

1 tsp sugar

1 tsp cornflour

1 tbsp sherry (optional)

1 lettuce

grated carrot or capsicum strips for garnish

METHOD

Put frying pan or wok on high heat. Add 1 tablespoon oil and quickly cook onions, garlic and ginger. After 1 minute pour in soya sauce and sesame oil. When the onions start to brown, toss in pork and stir-fry until it changes colour, stirring constantly (about 2 minutes). Remove mixture and set aside.

Put remaining oil in pan or wok and stir-fry mushrooms, 1 minute. Then add water chestnuts and fry 1 minute. Then bamboo shoots, to just warm through, 30 seconds. Remove from heat.

Stir sugar and cornflour in sherry (or 1 tablespoon water) until well mixed. Pour into pan or wok and stir with mushrooms, bamboo shoots and water chestnuts. Return to heat and mix well to allow mixture to thicken.

Stir onion/pork mixture into pan or wok to warm through. Wash individual leaves of lettuce, drain and dry with kitchen towel or paper.

Serve a generous dollop of mixture in a lettuce leaf, one or two per person, and top with garnish.

To eat: Roll lettuce leaf into a parcel and eat with fingers.

Pork Dim Sum

Steaming is one of the most efficient ways of cooking, keeping foods moist while the flavours are contained. This recipe is for little parcels of pork, vegetables and spices steamed over chicken consommé.

Serves 6

INGREDIENTS

300g lean pork (leg steak or schnitzel), finely minced
1/2 cup grated carrot
1/2 cup grated chinese cabbage
1 tbsp finely chopped onion
2 cloves garlic, finely chopped
1/2 tsp sesame oil
pepper
1 tbsp coriander, chopped finely
2 egg whites
24 wonton wrappers
1 litre low-salt chicken consommé (or chicken stock)
chopped spring onion and finely sliced capsicum for garnish

METHOD

In a mixing bowl combine the pork, vegetables, garlic, sesame oil, pepper and coriander.

In a separate bowl, whisk egg whites till stiff peaks form. Fold two-thirds of the egg white into the meat mixture, reserving the remaining egg white for sealing the parcels.

Spread out 12 wonton wrappers on clean surface, floured work bench or tea towel. Brush each one with egg white. Put a teaspoonful of mixture in centre of each wonton. Bring up sides and squeeze together to seal little parcels. Repeat with other 12 parcels.

Boil the chicken consommé. Place few wontons at a time on cabbage leaf in steamer and steam 15 minutes.

Serve in the chicken stock garnished with spring onion and capsicum.

Summer Sizzle

The barbecue has been the scene of many a gastronomic disaster, such as the first one I attended in this country back in 1971.

barbecuing has come a long way since the technique first acquired its name, possibly in the Caribbean where a method for curing meat on greenwood lattices over hot ashes was known as Boucan. The French called it boucanier and the Spanish barbacoa, which is close to the word with which we are all familiar.

Far from being the occasional social event it once was in Australia, this form of cooking has become part of our culinary routine, with the ubiquitous barbecue lit up with increasing frequency, both indoors and out.

Although the barbecue has fired us with so much enthusiasm, it also has been the scene of many a gastronomic disaster, such as the one I attended in this country back in 1971.

Fresh from England and wet behind the ears, I was invited to a barbecue held by some journalists with whom I had been working. "Bring some grog and a plate," they said, an odd request I thought. It was explained that by plate they meant my own meat. What strange form of hospitality it seemed to this European, that the only things provided by the hosts were their company and a venue.

However, not one to pass up the opportunity of eating al fresco, I went and bought a fabulous T-bone steak, at least 2 inches thick – it was inches in those days. It had a splendid fillet attached, certainly the finest example of the cut that I had seen. I anointed this treasure with oil, the best olive oil, some ground black

Fresh from England and wet behind the ears...

pepper, a little red wine (Australian, of course), some crushed garlic and some chopped thyme, then left it to marinate during the day.

My steak and I duly arrived at the party along with a splendid bottle of aged Henschke Hill of Grace, which was removed from me by the host at the door. I never saw it again. I was given a plastic cup and pointed in the direction of the backyard.

A splendid fire was burning in a split open 44 gallon drum and I looked forward to the incomparable flavours the wood-fired barbecue would give to the meat.

At an appointed time the barbecue fire was declared ready and in a trice a jostle of journalists threw a variety of foods on to the grill, lamb chops, sausages, and steaks.

I found a gap for my colossal cut and proudly laid it down, gently applying the marinade and I was soon caressed by the aromas of garlic, thyme and wine.

I moved away and continued the conversation I had been having about flies and the Aussie salute. I don't exactly know what happened then but I suspect someone had poured oil on the fire. Suddenly, there were sheets of flame followed by a pall of smoke. Party goers darted forward into the smoke with tongs, forks, anything that would enable them to retrieve their fare.

By the time I got to the scene only one thing remained on the barbecue, a morsel of charred meat which once could have been gravy beef, sirloin or porterhouse, it was hard to know. One thing I did know: it wasn't my T-bone.

Furious, I took the remaining blackened piece of shrivelled meat, put it on a cardboard plate, and went in search of the culprit. He turned out to be an ABC radio journalist who had already finished gobbling the fillet and had just started work on the other side of the bone, the juice running down his wretched chin. My juice.

"That's my steak," I petulantly protested. "It's a beauty," he gloated, talking with his mouth full. It's a sight I'll never forget.

I retreated, having to content myself with my charred remnant masked with tomato sauce and accompanied with a salad of iceberg lettuce and orange slices laced with a sweetened mayonnaise – made from a traditional recipe using condensed milk – a slice of what purported to be bread, and a plastic cup of flagon red wine.

I was consoled later with the fact that this reporter found himself transferred to some ghastly part of the world where the flies were even more numerous than ours, where journalists were uniformly despised, and where meat was as scarce as hen's teeth.

The other surprise I received at this, my maiden barbecue, was that the women did not attend the cooking. The only attendees were blokes, who trod a steady path between the two shrines of barbecue and keg.

Surprisingly, 25 years on, and in this age of emancipation and equal opportunity, women still do not get much of a guernsey at the barbecue, except for serving salads – oh, and of course washing up. But I have learnt much about this ancient form of dining:

Barbecue Tips

○ Don't use chipboard on the barbecue.
○ Don't rush to cook. Let the fire die down first.
○ Oil metal skewers before impaling the meat, fish or vegetable pieces.
○ When using satay sticks as skewers, soak them in water for an hour or so first.
○ Oil both sides of meat or fish before cooking.
○ Don't play with the food, turn once only.
○ Some vegetables cook well on the barbecue: eggplant, zucchini, tomatoes, for example. Brussels sprouts and broccoli do not.
○ Don't take your best wine.
○ Beware of thieving repatriated foreign correspondents with the initials NS!

> *To barbecue is a way of life rather than a desirable method of cooking.*
> **CLEMENT FREUD** *Freud on Food* 1978

"Poultry is for the cook what canvas is for the painter."

JEAN-ANTHELME BRILLAT-SAVARIN

Poultry

Chicken Pilau

A long time favourite of mine, which I've been preparing since I was a youth in the Dark Ages. Chicken was something of a luxury in those days, and as such, the chicken to rice ratio has changed somewhat in recent times. Skinless thigh meat is best for this dish, and I use the par-cooked Sungold rice which is easy to prepare with separate grains.

Serves 4

INGREDIENTS

2 large onions, thinly sliced
2 cloves garlic, finely chopped
1 tbsp olive oil
½ tsp sesame oil
1 tsp unsalted butter
400-500g skinless chicken
    thigh meat, cut into
    bite-size pieces
2 tsp ground coriander
½ tsp five spice powder
1 cup Sungold rice
500ml chicken stock
1 tbsp currants (optional)
2 tbsp cooked corn kernels
    (optional)
1 tbsp lightly toasted and
    finely chopped macadamia
    or pecan nuts
1 tbsp finely chopped
    coriander leaves (optional)

METHOD

In a heavy-based pan, sauté onions and garlic in olive oil, sesame oil and butter over medium heat until softened.

Put chicken, ground coriander and five spice powder in plastic bag and toss to coat. Add chicken to pan and sauté until just cooked. Add rice and cook until lightly browned.

Stir in stock and currants, cover pan and simmer for 15 minutes or until rice has absorbed the stock. Add corn, nuts and coriander leaves (if using).

Serving suggestion: Accompany Chicken Pilau with a tomato and cucumber salad.

Leftover potential: Keeps for a couple of days in the refrigerator. Refry to heat through before serving.

Chicken Pilau

Hunter Chicken

Deborah Whitebread's Cashew Pheasant

Chicken Pecan Terrine with
Onion and Citrus Chutney

Chicken Pecan Terrine with Onion and Citrus Chutney

Serves 8

METHOD
First prepare the capsicums by cutting slices of flesh away from the seeds and discarding the stalk. Place skin side up on an oiled baking tray. Grill until skin blackens.

Remove capsicum pieces from baking tray and place in a plastic bag. Tie top of bag and leave to cool. Once they are cool the skins are easily removed.

In a large bowl mix minced chicken, chopped pecan nuts, egg, onion, carrot, mixed spice, pepper, stock, juniper berries and brandy (if using). Mix well, then slowly add breadcrumbs to make a reasonably firm mixture.

Oil a 10 x 15cm terrine or other ovenproof dish and put down a layer of bacon rashers. Add one-third of the chicken mixture, packing down well on top of the bacon. Add a layer of whole pecans, followed by a layer of chicken strips. Add a layer of capsicum and repeat the whole process, finishing with a layer of the chicken mixture.

Cover dish with aluminium foil and stand in a roasting pan with enough water in it to come halfway up sides of the dish. Cook at 190°C for 2 hours.

Cool terrine completely then refrigerate before serving.

To make Onion and Citrus Chutney: Cook onions in oil over medium heat for about 5 minutes or until onions soften. Stir in sugar and keep cooking for about 10 minutes longer or until mixture starts to brown.

Add citrus fruit, orange juice, wine vinegar, coriander, ginger and pepper. Continue cooking, uncovered, until mixture reaches a jam-like consistency. Check that the chutney is not too sharp and, if it is, add more sugar. Allow to cool.

Leftover potential: Keeps for a week in the refrigerator.

INGREDIENTS
3 or 4 red or yellow capsicums
250g skinless chicken breast or thigh meat, minced or finely chopped
50g pecan nuts, finely chopped
1 large egg, lightly beaten
1 medium onion, finely chopped
1 small carrot, grated
1 tsp mixed spice
1/2 tsp black pepper
2 tbsp strong chicken stock
5 or 6 juniper berries, finely chopped (optional)
1 tbsp brandy (optional)
breadcrumbs
3 or 4 bacon rashers, rind and fat removed
50g whole pecan nuts
250g skinless chicken breast, cut into strips

Chutney
2 medium onions, finely chopped
1 tbsp oil
1/4 cup sugar
1 cup orange segments, cumquat slices or canned mandarin pieces
juice of 1 orange
2 tbsp good wine vinegar
1/2 tsp ground coriander
1/2 tsp ground ginger
pinch of pepper

Hunter Chicken

Mushrooms, onions and wine form the basis of the classic French sauce, Chasseur – or hunter – sauce, so-called because this sauce works extremely well with any game meat. It also goes beautifully with chicken, as in the Consuming Passions *Hunter Chicken recipe. I allow a maryland cut of chicken per person – that's the thigh and drumstick.*

Serves 4

INGREDIENTS

4 chicken maryland pieces, skinned

2 tbsp olive oil

2 tbsp brandy

4 tbsp chopped onions (preferably shallots)

150g chopped mushrooms (preferably wild)

500ml veal or chicken stock

300ml white wine (preferably chardonnay)

2 bay leaves

1-2 sprigs thyme

1-2 sprigs parsley

2 tsp tomato paste

METHOD

Brown chicken pieces in 1 tablespoon oil in a large saucepan over high heat.

Warm the brandy and flame the chicken. Once the flames have died down, remove chicken pieces, add onion and cook for 5 minutes. Remove onion and set aside.

Put remaining oil in pan, add mushrooms and cook for 2 minutes. Toss them around, and if they get too dry don't add any more oil. Instead, just add a little stock, making sure the mushrooms don't start stewing. Remove mushrooms.

Into the pan put the stock, wine and herbs (tied together with butcher's string). Add the tomato paste and reduce liquid until syrupy and about half its original volume.

Return chicken, onions and mushrooms to pan. Cover, reduce the heat and cook very, very, very slowly for about 1 hour.

Serving suggestion: Serve Hunter Chicken with plain noodles and a dark green vegetable.

Leftover potential: Hunter Chicken keeps well in the refrigerator for two or three days.

Deborah Whitebread's Cashew Pheasant

Deborah Whitebread is a creative young chef from London. Although she designed this for pheasant, you could use chicken breast.

Serves 4

INGREDIENTS

4 pheasant breasts, skin off
   and wing bone left on
2 green chillies, seeds
   removed and finely
   chopped
1 tsp aromatic salt or $1/2$ tsp
   sea salt
1 tsp ground cumin
200g cottage cheese
pepper to taste
400g raw onion
200g raw cashew nuts
200g natural yoghurt
200ml milk
$1/2$ tsp saffron

Aromatic salt

100g sea salt
1 tsp each of ground
   cinnamon and turmeric
1 tsp allspice
$1/2$ tsp ground fenugreek
1 tsp dried mint
2 tbsp ground almonds

METHOD

Make a pocket in each breast with a sharp knife. Blend the chillies with the salt until smooth. Add the cumin and cottage cheese. Season with a grinding of pepper. Fill the breasts with the mixture using a piping bag. Set aside.

Mince the onions and cashew nuts in a food processor until smooth. Add the yoghurt and milk, and mix. Pour into a deep, wide pan, add the saffron and heat.

Just before the milk starts to boil, add the breasts and allow to simmer very, very gently for about 15-20 minutes, turning halfway through. Don't let it boil!

To make the aromatic salt: Blend all the ingredients with a mortar and pestle or use a food processor.

Serving suggestion: On a bed of rice with sweet potatoes and spinach.

Chicken Involtini

This is a chicken version of an Italian veal dish. This recipe is one for chicken breast – allow one per person.

Serves 4

INGREDIENTS

4 full chicken breasts removed
    from the bone
1 tbsp olive oil, plus extra for
    frying involtini
2 cloves garlic, chopped
50g low fat mozzarella
    cheese, grated
1 tsp chopped fresh rosemary,
    sage or oregano
black pepper, to taste
grated nutmeg, to taste
flour
½ cup white wine
½ cup chicken stock

METHOD

Trim the fat from the breasts, remove the smaller of the two muscles and chop to use in the filling.

Make each breast into two larger flatter pieces by placing between two pieces of baking paper and bashing it with a rolling pin.

Into a pan place olive oil (extra virgin is best) and add the chopped garlic, then the chopped pieces of chicken breast. It only needs a couple of minutes to cook.

Take the pan off the heat and stir in the grated mozzarella cheese, sprinkle with the herbs, pepper, and nutmeg.

Place this mixture on to one side of the breast put the other side on top and tie it up or secure with a satay stick.

Roll the involtini in flour and fry in a little olive oil for five minutes, as the filling is already cooked. Remove from pan. Deglaze the pan with the wine and stock, reduce it to thicken. Pour over the chicken breast and serve with plain rice and a green salad.

Chicken Macadamia Nut Soufflé

There are few foods native to Australia that have made an impression on the rest of the world. One has, in a big way: The macadamia nut. Used in conjunction with chicken and a steamed choux pastry dough, it makes a dish that is nothing short of magnificent.

Serves 4

INGREDIENTS

2 cups water
125g butter
1½ cups self-raising flour
7 eggs
100g macadamia nuts
2 tsp oil
2 medium onions, finely diced
250g chicken breast, cut into strips
2 tbsp white wine
salt and pepper

METHOD

Make up a choux paste by boiling 2 cups of water and adding butter. Stir well and toss in the flour, stirring quickly. Cook over low heat for a couple of minutes.

Incorporate eggs one at a time, stirring constantly until mixture comes away from the side of the pan into a firm dough ball. Set aside.

Roughly chop macadamia nuts and lightly brown in pan with the oil over medium heat. They should be golden brown rather than black brown. Add onions and sweat for two or three minutes until they have softened. Add the chicken and continue cooking for two or three minutes, evaporating surplus liquid. Add wine and stir, still cooking gently; add salt and pepper to taste.

Fold the chicken/nut mixture into the choux paste.

Oil the inside of four 150ml ramekins or coffee cups. Put dollops of the mixture into each cup, coming no higher than two-thirds of the way up to allow for expansion.

Stand cups in large pan of about 3cm of boiling water, so that the water comes about half way up the cups. Cover and allow soufflés to steam for 20 minutes.

Christmas Present, Christmas Past

At certain times of the year I find that I'm dreaming of a grey Christmas, just like the ones I used to know, when I was growing up in England.

isn't life full of little mysteries? For example, when huge jet aircraft are parked on perfectly level airport aprons, why are chocks put against the wheels? Are these flying heavyweights really going to roll somewhere?

And how about sheep? In drier parts of our great brown land, sheep are desperate for good grazing, while the suburbs are full of lush green lawns which need valuable water, and which demand cutting on a regular basis. Sheep would be perfect.

Why do we insist on importing huge amounts of food into this country to the detriment of our own producers? We import bread and water. It's true. Stale foreign bread comes in as croutons, and we still are subjected to heavily branded mineral waters in restaurants.

A most important conundrum for this passionate consumer is why we ignore turkeys most of the year and then get a passion for them at Christmas time, when many of us insist on eating a traditional northern European Christmas lunch or dinner at the hottest time of year.

I confess I do it too, but then I have a valid excuse. It is all down to nostalgia. At certain times of the year I find that I'm dreaming of a

grey Christmas, just like the ones I used to know, when I was growing up in England. White ones were something of a luxury.

I'm not talking about presents, you can keep them. Nor the tinsel, the lights, and the fairy impaled on the Christmas tree, you're welcome to them too. No, for me the most perfect pleasure of Christmas is preparing for it in the kitchen.

I love spending hours in my inner sanctum, making pastry for biscuits and pies, creating the two differently flavoured stuffings for the turkey – one herbed and one spiced – and savouring the aromas of the ingredients of the pudding, dried fruits, citrus, beer and cognac.

Once I used to enjoy making my own mincemeat, after I'd researched its origins. I discovered that once upon a time mincemeat was exactly that, beef minced and mixed with fruits to help preserve it, so that the mince pies in olden times were more a savoury food.

These days, the only remaining animal component in the mincemeats you buy is beef suet.

Most of my best memories come from the time spent with my mother in my late teens when, over glasses of very dry sherry and chocolate rum truffles, we would talk about things such as the contribution science had made to the art of cooking turkey.

What particularly would amuse us was researcher Fick's Law, 'that the time taken for the centre of a spherical turkey to reach a given temperature is proportional to the square of the radius of the turkey'. And we'd laugh at the thought of Fick shopping for the perfect ball-shaped turkey.

It would always be the time to reminisce about embarrassing moments of Christmases past: Grandma falling asleep in the middle of a sentence, Auntie Vera flaming the pudding, and the tablecloth, with too much enthusiasm and spirit. We'd laugh and we'd cry

chopping onions for the stock we'd use later for gravy. We'd bake batches of buttery shortbread. We'd ice the cake. Late on Christmas Eve we'd set the table for the big family lunch (at which politics were not to be discussed).

Then we'd walk to the village church for midnight mass, a shambolic affair reminiscent of a scene from the *Vicar of Dibley*, with most of the parishioners looking a little the worse for wear and the bucolic vicar looking little better.

On Christmas Day, celebrations would begin at 11am sharp, with champagne and cheese and nut biscuits straight from the oven, good English cheeses, and orange glazed ham carved from the bone, while we opened the presents and gave thanks.

Then the firework display that was lunch. Oohs, aahs, gasps...

Soon the culmination of our labour of love was gone, in what seemed like a flash – or rather the bang of a Christmas cracker.

And as soon as lunch was over, my mother and I would be discussing what we'd do with the leftovers, while my father would retire to another place to rattle the furniture with his snoring.

Is it any wonder that with the temperature nudging the old century, I still enjoy the cold comfort provided by the ghosts of Christmases past.

> *Heaped up on the floor were turkeys, geese, game, poultry, brawn, great joints of meat, sucking pigs, long wreaths of sausage, mince-pies, plum-puddings, barrels of oysters, red-hot chestnuts, cherry-cheeked apples, juicy oranges, luscious pears, immense twelfth-cakes, and seething bowls of punch that made the chamber dim with their delicious steam.*
>
> **CHARLES DICKENS** *A Christmas Carol* **1843**

Roast Turkey with Two Stuffings

My preferred way of preparing the Christmas turkey is with two stuffings, one meat based, seasoned with spice and brandy, the other breadcrumb based, flavoured with herbs and lemon.

Serves a mob!

INGREDIENTS

roasting turkey with giblets
   removed
olive oil

Spicy meat stuffing

1 kg pork and veal mince (or
   sausage meat)
1 tsp mixed spice
1 tbsp brandy or cognac
250g rindless bacon, finely
   chopped
2 eggs
1/4 tsp salt and pepper

Lemon and herb stuffing

1 large onion, finely chopped
rind of a large lemon, grated
1 tbsp olive oil
1 tbsp chopped parsley
1 tbsp chopped thyme
1 heaped teaspoon minced
   garlic
1/2 cup hot chicken stock
fresh breadcrumbs

METHOD

To make spicy meat stuffing: Mix all ingredients in a large bowl.

To make lemon and herb stuffing: Mix all ingredients except breadcrumbs. When mixed, sprinkle in breadcrumbs and keep stirring until the mixture has a firm mashed potato consistency.

To prepare the turkey:
Wipe cavities fore and aft with paper towel. Stuff the larger cavity with the meat stuffing and the smaller cavity with the herb stuffing. Pull skin over stuffing and secure with satay sticks. Rub turkey with olive oil. Turn turkey over so that the breast is underneath.

Place on oiled baking tray and roast in oven at 180°C for 20 minutes per 500g (include weight of stuffing). Forty minutes before serving, turn bird over to brown breast. Twenty minutes before serving, remove turkey from oven and allow to stand until ready to carve.

Important hint: Turkey should be stuffed as close as possible to cooking time to avoid bacterial build-up.

Chicken Prawn Fandango

Chicken Prawn Fandango

METHOD

Cut chicken into bite-size pieces and sprinkle with szechuan pepper. Set aside.

Peel prawns. Put shells and heads in a saucepan and cover with water. Simmer gently for about 10 minutes to make a stock. Clean prawns and remove digestive tract by cutting along back and washing out any traces of black. Pat dry.

Grind together chilli, garlic, ginger, spring onions and coriander seeds and leaves.

Put one tablespoon peanut or olive oil and the sesame oil in a wok or large frying pan and stir-fry chicken over high heat for 4-5 minutes. Remove and set aside.

Stir-fry prawns for about 1 minute, adding more oil if necessary. Add capsicum and stir-fry for 30 seconds. Remove mixture. Add remaining oil and fry spice mixture for 30 seconds. Strain prawn stock and pour 3-4 tablespoons into pan. Stir well. Remove pan from heat and add coconut milk.

Add chicken, prawns and capsicum strips to pan and simmer over low heat for 5-6 minutes. Just before serving, stir in extra spring onions and capsicum strips and sprinkle with chopped coriander leaves.

Serving suggestion: Serve with rice.

Leftover potential: Keeps well and may be reheated or eaten cold.

The Spanish acknowledge it with their paella, as do the Chinese with a variety of dishes – that chicken combines well with seafood, as it does in this colourful concoction. Though the fandango is a Spanish dance, this dish owes more to Oriental cuisine.

Serves 4

INGREDIENTS

300g skinless, boned chicken
   leg meat
1/2 tsp szechuan pepper
400g green king prawns
1 tsp chopped or minced chilli
1 tsp chopped or minced garlic
1 tsp finely chopped or minced
   ginger
1 tbsp chopped spring onions,
   white parts only
1 tsp coriander seeds
1 tbsp coriander leaves
2 tbsp peanut or light olive oil
1 tsp sesame oil
1 tbsp thin strips of red
   capsicum
1 tbsp thin strips of yellow
   capsicum
2 tbsp coconut milk
chopped spring onions,
   capsicum strips and
   coriander

Chicken Potato Pie

A variation of the old-fashioned favourite, shepherd's pie, but this time using chicken.

Serves 6

INGREDIENTS

1 kg potatoes, peeled and
  chopped into large pieces
2 tbsp olive oil
2 thin young leeks, (finely
  sliced)
500g boned chicken thigh,
  (skinned and cut into
  bite-sized pieces)
1 or 2 rashers bacon cut into
  strips
1 tsp mixed spices
1 tbsp plain flour
2 tbsp chicken stock
1 tbsp each fresh oregano and
  thyme (or ½ tsp dried
  mixed herbs)
1 cup frozen peas (optional)
200g button mushrooms,
  (sliced)
2 tbsp milk plus 1 tbsp extra
¼ tsp white pepper
½ tsp grated nutmeg
1 egg yolk for glaze

METHOD

Bring a large quantity of lightly salted water to the boil then simmer potatoes until thoroughly cooked.

In a large frying pan, heat 1 tablespoon oil and cook the leeks gently for about 6 minutes, stirring them occasionally to break up the rings. Add the chicken pieces and bacon rashers and cook for a further 4 minutes. Add spice and flour and cook for a further 2 minutes stirring constantly. Add chicken stock and herbs and cook until the mixture has thickened. Stir in the frozen peas (if using). Place mixture in casserole dish.

In remaining oil, cook mushrooms, adding a little stock if they begin to stick. Add to the meat mixture.

Mash the potatoes with a little milk, white pepper and nutmeg. Spread mashed potato over meat and mushroom mixture, glaze top with egg yolk mixed with one tablespoon extra milk.

Bake in 190°C oven for about 35 minutes or until the top has browned nicely.

Yellow Rice and Chicken

One of the world's greatest culinary marriages is the one between chicken and rice, a splendid combination of protein and carbohydrate. This recipe is based on hameen, a dish traditionally prepared by Sephardic or Eastern Jews.

Serves 4

INGREDIENTS

8 boned chicken thighs,
    skinned and trimmed
2 tsp turmeric
2 tbsp extra virgin olive oil
seeds from 8 cardamom pods
2 small carrots, finely diced
3 cloves garlic, finely chopped
1 cup long grain rice
2 large tomatoes skinned and
    chopped
2 cups low salt chicken stock
    (or 1 cup canned tomatoes)
1 tsp turmeric (see hint)

METHOD

Toss chicken with 2 teaspoons turmeric in plastic bag. Heat 1 tablespoon olive oil and brown chicken all over. Remove and drain.

Remove cardamom seeds from pod by crushing pod with the back of a spoon.

In the remaining oil cook carrots with cardamom seeds and garlic for 5 minutes. Add rice and continue cooking for 5 minutes.

Cut chicken into small pieces and add to rice mixture. Add tomatoes, stock and additional teaspoonful of turmeric (optional).

Cover and simmer very slowly for 25 minutes, until rice is cooked.

Hint: The traditional recipe calls for lots of turmeric, but if you prefer less, disregard this last teaspoonful.

Are You Being Served?

I have to confess that I am obsessed with the need to eat and drink well. It's an aim that requires the cooperation of restaurateur, waiter – and customer.

how often has this happened to you? Your party is leaving the restaurant, you've paid, and on the way out you're asked: "How did you enjoy the meal?"

"It was fine," you reply.

Once outside, the conversation goes something like this:

"That was bloody terrible."

"Food was awful."

"So was the service."

"And how about charging us $18 for bread."

"And what about $38 for that wine. It's less than 10 bucks in a liquor store."

"And the MUSIC!"

"Never again!"

Of course we've all done it. There is always an element of risk when eating out. It can be expensive. And disappointing.

I have to confess that I am obsessed with the need to eat and drink well.

Forgive me if I'm Mr Fussy, but while the majority of the population seem comfortable with triple cheeseburgers, I do have trouble handling soggy, fat-sodden buns containing shreds of iceberg lettuce and chunks of oversalted minced meat seasoned with sugary tomato ketchup or fake mayonnaise, and accompanied with a fizzy brown drink made with sugar, water and by-products of the petroleum industry.

No, I need real food. Take away the fast food and give me the slow any day – or night, coupled with ambience and service.

Waiting for the best… fearing the worst…

Restaurants certainly have come a long way since that joke known as nouvelle cuisine was perpetrated on us – whose chief beneficiary was the New Zealand kiwi fruit industry. The fashion for smaller portions on larger plates, frequently accompanied by chunks of fruit, went so far that one restaurant I patronised chose to accompany each main course – whether it was meat, fish or seafood – with a whole plum, complete with the greasy fingerprints of a kitchen worker. Asked to explain this odd appearance on the plate, a waiter snapped at me: "It's noo-vell coo-zeen."

Another curse of this nouvelle cuisine era was alfalfa sprouts – still occasionally with us – tasting more of the fridge than anything else.

And in the early days of the trend, it was not just the food that had gone nouvelle, so it seemed had the service. In many restaurants the Maitre 'd appeared to have disappeared, to be replaced by a new phenomenon with such titles as Customer Relations Manager. This breed of creature, which unfortunately did not die out with the cuisine, displayed a sort of insincere, plastic charm that carried with it a kind of glib monologue usually along the lines of: "Hello, I'm Wendy, your customer relations manager and I'll be looking after you tonight, if there is anything you need, please do not hesitate to ask – blah – blah -blah... Have a nice meal."

She would then reappear after each mouthful of food to ask if everything was all right, but was never there when a customer actually needed anything.

At the end of one memorable meal, where the service had been fawning but inefficient, I was asked by the highly perfumed, coiffed and manicured CRM if I had enjoyed the meal.

I answered that yes, the food had been good, but the service had been obsequious, she responded, "Thank you, we do try to please."

Also appearing in plague proportion around this time – and also still with us – are the Mr and Ms Huffy kind of waiters – or should that be unkind of waiters – who think restaurants would be far better places without customers.

I am reminded that on one disastrous occasion I asked a Huffy what was the Plat du Jour on the menu, to which he snapped, "It's the dish of the day."

The Huffies can be recognised by the way they appear to look round the restaurant but without actually seeing anyone who needs attention. They are likely to drum their pencils on their note pads while waiting to take the order, will sigh if you need longer to consider, and are unlikely to know what the vegetables of the day are.

When topping up the wine glasses, instead of evenly sharing out the wine, they will fill all but one glass and then ask if another bottle of wine is required. Their numbers seem to have grown in epidemic proportions.

Waiters of whatever sex acquired the ridiculous title of waitpersons.

Among them came the Space Invaders, waiters who approach the table, kneel at your feet as though about to propose – or even pull up a chair and join you – to explain the establishment's many specials. They usually greet the customer with "Hi", and when placing the meal before you, they will say: "There ya go."

Talented chefs and waiters can now be found throughout the country and the local produce is getting better all the time. So what can we all do to make eating out the pleasurable experience it should be?

Success relies on the cooperation of restaurateurs, chefs, waiters – and customers. I've surveyed members of each group to come up with the following rough guide.

> **The golden rule when reading a restaurant menu is, if you can't pronounce it you can't afford it.**
>
> **FRANK MUIR** *English humourist*

Tips for Waiters

○ Regard your job as an important one. It is. The customers are dependent on you to make their meal enjoyable. And remember who's paying your wages – they are (even if you think they are not paying enough).

○ Know what foods you serve, and what are the vegetables and salads of the day.

○ Over-familiarity is out, customers don't need to know you're Simon or Claire.

○ Don't refer to yourself as a waitperson. Male or female, you're a WAITER.

○ Treat women as you would men. Don't give them the worst tables and the most sluggish service. Don't rush them through their meals, either.

○ Try not to develop waiter blindness, appearing to look but not actually seeing customers who need attention.

○ Dishes are served with capsicuM not capsicuN, bruschetta is pronounced brusKetta. And it's not an aDvocado.

○ Serve without surliness. Don't be an arrogant, impatient pencil-tapper.

○ When placing food on the table, try to avoid saying "There ya go!"

○ The music is for the patrons, not the waiters.

Cooks' Endeavours

○ Try making real stock, avoid flavouring with boosters, especially containing MSG.

○ Make real mayonnaise, never serve mayonnaise out of a 44-gallon drum (it's likely to be high in sugar). And avoid making tartare sauce using commercial mayonnaise as a base.

○ Please, no orange twists or alfalfa in salads.

○ No imported croutons.

○ Avoid serving unripe tomatoes.

○ Salads. If you're calling them by their proper name (Waldorf, Caesar or Niçoise) make them properly. And don't cheat. A mountain of iceberg lettuce topped with a few pieces of squid and pretend crab meat is not a seafood salad.

○ You should be able to eat what's on the plate so don't garnish with anything inedible.

○ Avoid purple prose in menus. If it's 'lamb chop and mash with gravy' don't call it 'Selected choice-cut of grass fed, sensitively killed, new season's lamb, pan seared to perfection, then delicately simmered in wine-laden jus and thoughtfully served atop a soft mound of puréed pommes de terres seasoned with newly dried rosemary leaves and unselfishly accompanied with a sublime savoury sauce-brune.'

○ Breads. Spare us the 'focaccia' that in reality is a flattened white loaf topped with dried mixed herbs.

Restaurateurs

○ The customer is always right, even when he or she is not.

○ Make it clear whether or not table service is provided, or whether you have to do anything awkward, such as order at the counter, take your coffee to the table with you, have your food served by a waiter, and then pay at the counter. There are so many variations in Australia it's no wonder visitors have no idea what's going on.

○ Avoid spelling mistakes on your menus. It simply indicates sloppiness.

○ Don't pressure customers to have more wine than they need or want.

○ Avoid over complex menus. Too much choice places strain on customers.

○ Discourage use of too many specials. Sometimes it's like being given an oral memory test.

○ Treat your chefs and waiters with respect.

○ Don't deafen patrons with music, and then ignore requests to turn it down.

- Avoid Kenny Gee CDs.
- Avoid ridiculous job titles, such as Customer Relations Manager.

Customers

- Book your table in advance if possible and notify the restaurant of any changes in numbers of diners.
- Always let the restaurant know if you can't keep your booking. It's not just bad manners, it's grossly unfair to restaurateurs to just not bother turning up. They may have turned customers away.
- Turn off the mobile phone.
- Bill splitting. It's a sensitive issue. Let the restaurant know in advance if you want to do it. Restaurants may allow bill splitting if they're given notice and they're not desperately busy.
- If a dish is not to your satisfaction, say so immediately, don't plough through it and then complain later.
- By all means, ask for a recommendation of a wine to go with the meal. Most restaurants will be happy to help and won't rip you off. But watch out if you're offered that special wine that's not on the wine list.
- Make sure the bottle is opened at the table so you know what you're getting.
- Allow someone on your table to try the wine. And don't forget you're looking for faults in the wine so don't send it back just because it's not to your taste.

Tasting food in the Perth Hyatt kitchen.

- If having a second bottle of the same wine, check that it too is not corked.
- Tipping. Ask the restaurateurs and they'll likely tell you waiters are adequately paid. Certainly, they are compared with some countries, where waiters rely on tips to earn a living. But they work hard for the money they get and good service deserves recognition with a tip, especially if the restaurant has been very busy, and they've done a good job.
- Treat waiters with respect.
- Always get someone to check the bill.
- If asked whether the meal was enjoyed, tell the truth!

Avoid any restaurant where a waiter arrives with a handful of knives and forks just as you reach the punchline of your best story and says 'Which of you is having the fish?'

JOHN MORTIMER *The Observer* 1978

Duck Couscous

Serves 4

INGREDIENTS

2 duck breasts

1 tbsp soy sauce

1 tsp sesame oil

½ tsp five spice

Sauce

100g abalone mushrooms

100g shiitake mushrooms

100g field mushrooms

1 tbsp oil

150ml sherry

150ml chicken or veal stock,
    thickened with a little
    cornflour

Couscous

500ml water

125g instant couscous

1 tsp oil

40g unsalted butter

METHOD

Make several cuts diagonally across the skin side of the duck breasts, taking care not to cut right through. Mix up all the other ingredients and rub well into the skin of the duck. Allow to stand for at least 10 minutes or leave overnight. Drain the liquid and reserve the marinade for sauce. (See hint.)

Sear the breasts in a hot non-stick pan over medium heat for 2-3 minutes each side. Place on a rack on a baking tray and cook in a hot oven, at least 220°C for approximately 8 minutes for rare, longer for medium. Much of the fat will drain off during this process. Remove from the oven and allow to settle in a warm place.

To make the sauce: Quickly pan-fry the mushrooms in the oil until just cooked. Do not let them stew. Remove from the pan and keep in a warm place.

Deglaze the pan with sherry and allow to reduce a little before adding the thickened stock. Cook over a medium heat for a few minutes to further reduce.

Hint: The leftover marinade from the duck may be added to this sauce while it is reducing.

To make the couscous: Boil the water. Add the oil. While stirring, sprinkle in the couscous. Cover, reduce heat and allow to simmer for a few minutes. Add the butter and fluff up with a fork.

Slice the duck breasts. Put the couscous on a warm dish, stir the mushrooms through the sauce, and add to the couscous. Then top with duck pieces and serve.

Whitsunday Quail

Hayman Island chef, Mark Patten, cooked up a storm with barbecued quail served with pickled vegetables.

Serves 4

INGREDIENTS

2 tsp finely chopped red chilli
1 tsp finely chopped green chilli
1 tsp finely chopped ginger
1 tsp finely chopped garlic
1 tsp finely chopped coriander root
3 tsp hoisin sauce
3 tsp light soy sauce
4 quail, jointed (leave the skin on)

Pickled vegetables

2 sticks lemon grass stem, crushed
1 tbsp coriander root
2 red chillies, sliced
1 piece galangal root
1 tbsp coriander leaves
200ml mirin
200ml rice wine vinegar
1 tbsp palm sugar
2 capsicums, finely sliced
1 cucumber, peeled, seeded and finely sliced
2 tbsp sliced bok choy

METHOD

Mix all the marinade ingredients and stir in the quail pieces. Leave to marinate. When ready, barbecue the quail until cooked through.

To make the pickled vegetables: Mix all the pickling ingredients together and bring to the boil. Remove from the heat and add the vegetables – capsicum, cucumber and bok choy. Refrigerate for at least 6 hours.

Serving suggestion: Serve the hot barbecued quail with salad greens and the pickled vegetables.

Chicken Masala

Garam masala is one of the great Indian spice combinations.

Serves 4

INGREDIENTS

750g skinless chicken thigh
   pieces on the bone
2 tsp turmeric
2 tbsp olive oil
1 onion, finely chopped
2 tsp minced garlic
2 tsp minced ginger
2 tbsp chopped coriander
   leaves
1 tbsp chopped mint leaves
1 tsp ground fenugreek
2 tbsp Thai-style sweet chilli
   sauce
1 tbsp garam masala
1 cup chicken stock
½ cup coconut cream
1 tamarind fruit, peeled and
   soaked in 2 tbsp hot water
   (optional) or 1 tbsp lemon
   juice (also optional)
coriander leaves and toasted
   peanuts for garnish

Garam masala

4 or 5 cardamom pods
2 tsp coriander seeds
2 tsp cumin seeds
1 tsp black peppercorns
½ nutmeg, grated
6 or 7 cloves
4cm cinnamon stick, broken
   into pieces

METHOD

Put chicken and turmeric in a plastic bag and toss to coat. Sauté chicken in a little olive oil for 2-3 minutes over medium heat to brown, then remove from pan.

In same pan, sauté onion, garlic and ginger in a little more oil for 4-5 minutes.

Add coriander leaves, mint, fenugreek, chilli sauce, garam masala, stock, coconut cream and tamarind pulp or lemon juice (if using). Add chicken and simmer very slowly for 45 minutes.

To make garam masala: Remove seeds from cardamom pods. Put cardamom seeds and other spices in coffee grinder or mortar and grind to make a powder. Sift through a sieve and regrind any large pieces. Store in an airtight container. (The mixture keeps very well for several weeks).

Serving suggestion: Serve on a bed of rice, garnished with coriander leaves and peanuts.

Leftover potential: This dish is even better the next day. Keeps for 2 or 3 days in the refrigerator. Reheat before serving.

Apricot Chicken (or Pork)

An updated version of a Flemish recipe I used to enjoy as a boy. It's less rich than the original, even more tasty – and its name is much easier to say than Varkenslapjes met abrikoszen! It may also be prepared using pork chops.

Serves 4

INGREDIENTS

4 chicken thighs

1 egg

breadcrumbs

2 tbsp olive oil (or other frying medium low in saturated fat)

1 large can Australian apricot halves (825g)

1 medium onion, finely sliced

1 tbsp wine vinegar

1 cup (200ml) chicken stock (or vegetable stock)

1 tsp minced ginger

1 tsp minced garlic

1 tsp dijon mustard

black pepper

METHOD

Dip chicken thighs in the beaten egg and then in the breadcrumbs. Shake off excess crumbs. Fry in 1 tablespoon olive oil until browned, about 4 minutes each side. Remove chicken thighs from pan and put in shallow baking dish.

Drain apricots and chop up all except eight halves.

In the pan used to brown the pork, cook the onion slices in 1 tablespoon oil until soft, about 5 minutes at medium heat.

Put all other ingredients except 8 apricot halves into the pan. Stir and reduce over high heat until you have a sauce of syrupy consistency.

Pour sauce over chicken pieces. Top with remaining apricots, sprinkle lightly with breadcrumbs, season with black pepper and place in oven at 160°C for 45 minutes.

Serving suggestion: I like to serve this dish sprinkled with chopped spring onions and accompanied by mashed potatoes and green vegetables.

Chicken Waterzooi

Based on the national dish of Belgium, this chicken casserole benefits from the addition of one of the world's most useful fruits, the lemon.

Serves 4

INGREDIENTS

4 chicken maryland pieces, skinned
750ml low-salt chicken stock
1 medium onion, chopped finely
small sprig parsley
small sprig thyme
2 bay leaves
3 juniper berries, crushed
½ tsp grated nutmeg
2 sticks celery, sliced
2 young leeks, sliced
2 medium carrots, grated
2 cloves garlic, finely chopped
2 egg yolks, lightly beaten
1 tbsp cornflour
1 tsp dijon mustard
juice and grated rind of 1 large lemon

METHOD

In a large saucepan, put chicken pieces, stock, onion, herbs, juniper berries, nutmeg and half the celery, leeks and carrots. If the stock does not cover ingredients, add water until all ingredients are covered and simmer for about 1 hour or until chicken falls off the bone.

Drain chicken and keep warm. Strain cooking liquid back into the saucepan. Add remaining celery, leeks, carrots, and garlic and cook, uncovered, for 30 minutes or until reduced to half the volume of strained liquid. Just before serving, remove chicken meat from bone.

Mix together egg yolks, cornflour and mustard. Slowly mix in lemon juice and rind.

Stir in reduced stock, a spoonful at a time, until about 500ml is added, then pour this mixture back into the reduced stock. Cook, stirring constantly, for about 1 minute, or until sauce thickens.

Arrange chicken on warm serving plates and pour over the thick sauce with its vegetables.

Serving suggestion: For a complete meal accompany with wholemeal rolls, or boiled rice or pasta.

Leftover potential: Keeps for two or three days in the refrigerator.

Grape Chicken Idea

Based on a Lebanese recipe, this dish combines the fruitiness of grapes, with the sourness of wine vinegar and a bold blend of herbs and spices.

Serves 4

INGREDIENTS

1 tbsp macadamia, walnut or
   almond oil
$1/2$ tsp ground cinnamon
$1/2$ tsp ground nutmeg
2 or 3 cloves
150g seedless grapes, washed
250ml fruity white wine
1 tbsp good white wine
   vinegar (or red wine vinegar
   for a darker sauce)
2 tbsp chicken stock
500g skinned and boned
   chicken thigh meat
1 tbsp finely chopped onion
2 tbsp almond meal
pepper to taste
2 tsp chopped fresh marjoram
   or thyme (or $1/2$ tsp dried
   thyme)
$1/4$ tsp chilli powder (optional)
1 or 2 tbsp blanched almonds
   to serve

METHOD

Heat oil in a frying pan over medium heat. Add cinnamon, nutmeg and cloves and sizzle for a few seconds. Remove cloves. Add whole grapes and cook for 2 minutes.

Add wine, vinegar and stock and cook for about 10 minutes, or until reduced by half.

Meanwhile, open out the chicken pieces and lay each on a length of butcher's (or other cotton) string. Top with a little of the onion, almond meal, pepper, marjoram or thyme and chilli powder, if using. Pat down. Roll up and tie each into a parcel, then nestle in the reduced sauce.

Sprinkle remaining almond meal and onion into the sauce. Cover pan and simmer very slowly for about 30 minutes, turning the parcels after 15 minutes. Dry toast the blanched almonds for about 1 minute over medium heat, or until just browned.

Once cooked, remove chicken and keep warm. Reduce sauce to a syrupy consistency over medium heat. Serve parcels with sauce and topped with blanched almonds.

Leftover potential: Keeps two or three days in the refrigerator.

"There is no love sincerer
than the love of food."

GEORGE BERNARD SHAW

Desserts

Iced Prune and Armagnac Parfait

Take two of my favourite ingredients and a recipe from one of my favourite chefs and you have the basis for a simply superb and indulgent dessert. The ingredients are prunes and Armagnac and the chef is Martin Webb. You could substitute Cognac for the Armagnac, or rum, or as a last resort, brandy. Warning – this is very much for occasional consumption as part of a well-balanced diet!

Serves 4-6

INGREDIENTS

6 egg yolks

140g caster sugar

450ml King Island Cream (or other double cream)

5 tbsp Armagnac

20cm sponge about 5cm thick

Conserve

450g pitted prunes (moist ones), coarsely chopped

125g caster sugar

100ml Armagnac

METHOD

To make the conserve: Combine the prunes and the 125g caster sugar and 250ml cold water in a saucepan. Bring to the boil, then lower heat and simmer gently until mixture is of a jam-like consistency.

Cool until just warm, then stir in Armagnac. Set aside. Put the egg yolks into a bowl and whisk. Reserve.

In a heavy-based saucepan, heat the 140g caster sugar with 140ml water and cook until mixture reaches the soft ball stage (112°C on a sweet thermometer).

Starting with tiny drips, whisk the sugar syrup into the egg yolks. When completely combined, set aside to cool.

Whisk the cream and as it starts to thicken, whisk in Armagnac. Continue whisking until soft peaks form.

When the egg and sugar mixture is cold, fold into the cream mixture and beat until soft peaks form.

Slice the sponge horizontally into two thin layers. Cover the base of a terrine or loaf tin with a layer of sponge (you can freeze the rest for later use). Sprinkle sponge with some of the liquid from the top of the prune conserve. Spread sponge with some of the prune conserve, then top with cream mixture. Bang the terrine on the work surface to remove air bubbles. Freeze overnight. Remove from freezer 2 minutes before serving.

To serve: Cut parfait into slices, using a knife that has been dipped in boiling water. Accompany with a little prune conserve on the side.

Left-over potential: Keeps for a few days in the freezer.

Iced Prune and Armagnac Parfait

Nightingales' Nests

Nightingales' Nests

An Australian version of a Turkish classic, Bulbul Yuvasi, it is a sort of curly nut strudel made with macadamia nuts. I find a thin rolling pin – or a piece of 2cm dowel – is best for making these nests.

Serves 8

METHOD

Mix macadamia nuts with caster sugar, cinnamon and lemon rind, if used.

Dampen a tea towel, shake off surplus water and put on work bench as a working surface for the pastry. Put pastry sheets on the tea towel (allowing 1 sheet per nest). Brush each sheet lightly with oil. Sprinkle about 1 tablespoon of the nut mixture evenly over the top sheet of pastry.

Put the rolling pin on a corner of the pastry, wrap a little of the top sheet of pastry over the rolling pin and roll up the sheet of pastry with the nut mixture on it. When it's rolled up, slide the roll off the rolling pin and curl it into snail-like shape. Repeat the process until all the pastry and mixture is used.

Put the pastries on an oiled baking tray. Bake at 180°C for 25-30 minutes or until browned. Check frequently as small nests may take less time to cook. While the nests are cooking, make the sauce.

To make the sauce: Dissolve sugar in water and boil for 15 minutes. Remove from heat, add lemon juice and spoon hot sauce over the cooked nests.

When cool, sprinkle with pistachio nuts and serve.

Leftover potential: This is best eaten the same day or the next day at the latest.

INGREDIENTS

200g macadamia nuts, finely chopped
1 tbsp caster sugar
1/4 tsp ground cinnamon
grated rind of lemon (optional)
light oil such as peanut or canola for brushing pastry
8 sheets of filo pastry
50g pistachio nuts, finely chopped, to garnish

Lemon Sauce

250g caster sugar
350ml water
1 tbsp lemon juice

Melon Surprise

I first discovered this extraordinarily easy but rewarding recipe as a child in Belgium.

Serves 6

INGREDIENTS
1 ripe rockmelon (cantaloupe)
juice of 2 lemons
caster sugar to taste
   (2 or 3 tbsp)
low-fat vanilla ice cream

METHOD
With the melon standing up on its stalk end, cut the top off about one-fifth way down the melon. Reserve tops. Scoop out melon seeds and clean up cavity.

Mix lemon juice and sugar and adjust to taste, allowing the mixture to be a little on the sharp side rather than too sweet.

Pour mixture into the melon. Replace the top. Place on a dish, wrap with plastic film and put in the refrigerator overnight. (It's best to seal the flavours inside plastic film since the smell of melon permeates.)

Next day, just before serving, remove the melon from fridge, pour juice into jug. Pack melon cavity with ice cream. Replace lid. Take to the table and serve immediately, cutting slices vertically through the melon.

Nashi Crunchie

A recent horticultural success story in Australia has been the nashi pear. It is said to have been introduced here in the 1800s by Chinese miners. I've adapted this dish from an apple crumble to make a crunchier dessert.

Serves 6

INGREDIENTS

3 large nashi pears

100ml orange juice

grated zest of 1 orange

3 or 4 tbsp brown sugar (light or dark)

1 tsp powdered cinnamon

1/2 tsp grated nutmeg

2/3 cup plain flour

100g butter

1/2 cup finely chopped macadamia nuts (or almonds)

METHOD

Chop nashi, skin included, into bite sized-pieces. Grease a baking dish. Put nashi in bottom of baking dish.

Pour over orange juice and sprinkle in the grated orange zest.

Now mix up the crunchie ingredients: Three or four tablespoons of brown sugar, half a teaspoon of powdered cinnamon, the grated nutmeg, and the plain flour. Cut in the butter and add the macadamias.

Now this is all rubbed together to make a crumbly mixture. Don't overwork it – it should remain light. Cover the nashi pears with this mixture.

Cover the dish and bake for half-an-hour at about 180°C. Then uncover it and cook for a further half hour.

Serving suggestions: Nashi Crunchie is bliss served with natural yoghurt dressing, as follows: Mix 150ml natural yoghurt, 2 tsp honey and the grated zest of 1/2 orange.

Talking Turkey

Many of the pastries have feminine names, such as dainty fingers, lips of the beauty, ladies navels and so on. And they taste as sweet as they sound.

4.30 am. The day was breaking. Actually, not so much breaking as gently hauling itself up behind the silhouetted Istanbul skyline. The sky was two dozen shades of red, like a palate of shepherds' warnings? The air was as still as a fish fillet and I was sitting on the hotel room balcony, lagged from a 16-hour flight from Australia, but bristling with the anticipation of my first sight of the Bosphorus – that great and furiously busy waterway which I was told the hotel overlooked – and the splendid mosques and minarets. Oh, and my first Turkish breakfast.

As the sun came up, imagine my surprise to find that the first things its light revealed were not the domed mosques and pointy minarets that I thought I was seeing in silhouette against the sky, but satellite dishes and radio masts. The Bosphorus itself was hidden beneath an old yellow grey blanket of smog, and rather than male voices calling the faithful to prayer – as I had been expecting – the only sounds were of cars and car horns. Istanbul holds the record for the most horn players performing together in any one place and apparently, there are so many vehicles in the city that it would be impossible for them all to be parked at any one time. There just isn't enough roadside. Or so the story goes.

A less hungry visitor might have been somewhat disenchanted by this first encounter with Turkey, but not this gastro-tourist. I was in Istanbul and I was here to eat. Well, mostly.

Three things I quickly learned that first morning: first, the Turks have forgiven us for having grabbed the 2000 Olympic Games from them. Second, it's easy to be a millionaire in Turkey where the rate of exchange means that one Australian dollar buys you around 8,000 Turkish lira – a million for just $125. Third, the food is magnificent.

Istanbul is unique in that it straddles two continents. Someone living in Asia could drive to work in Europe. It's called the crossroads of Europe and Asia, and that reflects its culinary complexity. With historic influences from the Orient and Byzantium, the intricacy further grew in the 1920s when Ataturk took power and attempted, with some success, to westernise the country.

Fortunately, the tradition was strong and the Turks still hang on to their old-fashioned ways. True, there are fast food outlets, but not in the way we know – and there's not a golden arch in sight. Instead flat pide bread is sold with kebab meat on the street. There are bagel and bread sellers wheeling their carts around. Drink vendors sell a sour cherry drink from elaborately decorated tanks on their backs.

Coffee was introduced into Europe via Turkey and the coffee shops are still a big feature of life, especially for the men. Small kebab restaurants too are always busy, alive with vigorous conversation, again a male preserve. During the evenings the men all seem to leave their families to eat together and drink, mostly Turkish tea, called chai. In fact tea is so fundamental to the city's psyche that I was given a cup both when I took my clothes into the tiny local laundry and when I collected them again. And on each occasion someone was sent out to get it.

The culinary heritage is rich. Numerous fish, meat, egg, rice and vegetable dishes are artfully prepared with dried fruits, nuts, spices, and herbs. Much food is char-grilled and is usually accompanied by yoghurt sauces. And beautifully sweet desserts and pastries are served with the most extraordinarily delicious Kaymak, a thick clotted cream – simply irresistible.

That all applied to breakfast which was laid out as a symphony of taste, colour and texture. Cold meats and fish dishes were served alongside massive bowls of fresh and dried fruit salads and the best thick yoghurt I have tasted, but the highlight was the oily flat Turkish bread and light bagels eaten with honey from a whole honeycomb and a dollop – no, make that two – of the heavenly cream.

Perhaps surprisingly croissants also were served. I say that because pastry is believed to have originated in Budapest in the 17th century, to celebrate the defeat of the Turks who were besieging the city. According to *Larousse Gastronomique*: 'Bakers working during the night heard the noise made by the Turks and gave the alarm. The assailants were repulsed and the bakers who had saved the city were granted the privilege of making a special pastry which had to take the form of a crescent in memory of the Ottoman flag.'

Many of the pastries are made with filo pastry, all are made with loving care and most have feminine names, such as dainty fingers, lips of the beauty, ladies navels and so on. And taste as sweet as they sound.

Istanbul: city of history and truly magnificent food.

Yoghurt is a big feature of the cuisine, thick and rich with just a touch of sourness. It is extensively used in soups and sauces – such as ravioli with garlic, mint, and paprika yoghurt sauce, as well as being applied to bread dough just before cooking.

In the few days in this fabulous city, with its constant throb of activity, I discovered a charming hospitable people with a passion for good food and while I did see the mosques and minarets, and the fabulous bazaar and the Topkapi Palace, and even had a trip on the Bosphorus, my firmest memory was of having been introduced to some of the finest gastronomic delights to have passed my lips.

And I did learn to say at least two words in Turkish: afiyet olsun – or Bon Appétit.

Sweet Baked Ricotta with Glazed Peaches

One of my favourite recipes from a favourite restaurant, this dish is by Genevieve Harris of Nediz Tu in Adelaide. Ricotta is baked into a loaf, cooled and served with peaches. It could also be used to accompany other soft fruits.

Serves 8

INGREDIENTS

800g ricotta cheese
2 eggs
1 vanilla bean (or 1 tsp vanilla
    essence)
225g icing sugar
8 ripe freestone peaches
extra icing sugar

METHOD

Preheat oven to 150°C.

Put ricotta cheese and eggs in a large bowl and whisk to combine. Split the vanilla bean lengthwise, scrape out the seeds and add to ricotta mixture (or add vanilla essence). Sift in icing sugar and mix thoroughly.

Line a non-stick 25cm loaf tin with a strip of non-stick baking paper, so that it runs along the bottom, up each end and extends out above the tin providing tabs to remove the ricotta when it has cooled.

Spoon the ricotta mixture into the tin and cover with foil. Put the tin in a larger baking dish and pour in enough water to come halfway up the sides of the tin.

Carefully put in the oven and bake for 40 minutes or until ricotta is firm.

When cooked, remove the loaf tin from the water bath and remove the foil. Cool, then cover with plastic film and refrigerate.

When cold, run a knife around the edge of tin to loosen the ricotta loaf and pull on tabs to remove. Slice and serve at room temperature.

For the glazed peaches: Halve the peaches, remove the stones and sprinkle cut sides with icing sugar. Put under a hot grill and grill for 2-5 minutes or until sugar caramelises.

Serving suggestion: Arrange two peach halves and a slice of ricotta on each serving plate. A peach syrup may be made by boiling peaches for 15 minutes in a water and sugar mixture. Drain and reduce the liquor over medium heat until syrupy.

Leftover potential: Baked ricotta will keep for several days in the refrigerator.

Noah's Pudding

Of all the dishes I've done on Consuming Passions, none has been such a curious combination of ingredients as is found in Noah's Pudding, probably so called because, like the ark, everything goes into it. It's a wholesome dessert which can be eaten for breakfast, lunch, tea or dinner.

Serves 12

INGREDIENTS

1 cup wheat (burghul)
1 cup medium grain calrose rice
500ml orange juice
100g sultanas
12 dried apricots
6 dried figs
2 tbsp honey
1 tsp rosewater
2 strips lemon rind
1 can white beans, drained and rinsed
1 can chick peas, drained and rinsed
200g mixed nuts (almonds, pine nuts, pistachio, hazelnuts)
300ml thickened natural low-fat yoghurt (see hint)

METHOD

Soak wheat in water overnight. Rinse and boil in water until soft (about one hour).

In another pan, boil rice in water until tender (about 25 minutes) .

Warm orange juice and soak dried fruits with honey, rosewater and lemon rind. Add wheat, rice, beans and chick peas. Refrigerate overnight.

Serve chilled or at room temperature, mixed with the nuts and topped with natural yoghurt.

Hint: To thicken yoghurt, put yoghurt in muslin-lined strainer and stand it over a bowl in the refrigerator overnight.

Panforte (Strong Bread)

Although this is a traditional Italian Christmas confection from Tuscany, it is perfect for any special occasion. Because there is quite a lot of work involved, I always make two at a time. For a darker, chocolate-flavoured panforte I add cocoa.

INGREDIENTS

200g raw hazelnuts, skin on

200g blanched almonds

50g raw macadamia nuts

200g citrus peel, chopped

100g dried figs, chopped

100g dried apricots, chopped

175g plain flour

2 tsp ground cinnamon

1/2 tsp ground coriander

1/2 tsp ground cloves

1/2 tsp grated nutmeg

1/2 tsp white pepper

2 tsp ground ginger

2 tbsp cocoa (optional)

500g sugar

250g honey

125g unsalted butter

METHOD

Roast hazelnuts at 200°C for 15 minutes. When hazelnuts are slightly cooled, wrap in a tea towel and rub off skins. (It doesn't matter if some skin remains).

Toast almonds in a dry pan until browned. Roughly chop the hazelnuts and almonds. It doesn't matter if some whole nuts remain. Roughly chop macadamia nuts.

Mix nuts with peel, figs, apricots, flour, cinnamon, coriander, cloves, nutmeg, pepper, ginger and cocoa (if using).

Grease two 28cm springform cake tins and line base and inner wall with non-stick baking paper.

In a saucepan, preferably non-stick, put sugar, honey and butter. Heat, stirring constantly, to 118°C on a sugar thermometer. If not using a sugar thermometer, keep cooking until mixture is smooth, bubbling fiercely, just starting to change colour, and reaches the soft ball stage.

Quickly stir sugar mixture into fruit mixture. Divide mixture between prepared tins. Press down with a wet spoon, dipping it into water every few seconds to stop sticking.

The mixture need not be spread evenly as it will soften and spread during cooking.

Bake at 160°C for 30 minutes. Allow to cool, then remove from tin. Remove baking paper from base. Sprinkle with icing sugar.

Keep quality: Will keep well in an airtight container (as long as your family and friends don't discover it!)

Hint: The soft ball stage is reached when a small amount of sugar mixture dropped into water will roll into a ball in your fingers.

Panforte

Kate Lamont's
Citrus Quinces

Fruit Flamri

Crème Brûlée

Crème Brûlée

*Sheer indulgence.
Literally translated from
the French as 'burned
cream', this rich dessert
is perfect served with
fresh summer fruits.
Prepared in individual
dishes, it is a custard
cream with a delightful
crunchy sugar topping.*

Serves 4

INGREDIENTS

75g caster sugar
3 large egg yolks (from 60g
   eggs)
300ml whipping cream
1 tsp vanilla essence
25g caster sugar, for tops

METHOD

Beat the sugar with the egg yolks until all the sugar has dissolved.
Heat cream in heavy saucepan until just boiled. Add vanilla
essence. Pour cream and vanilla into the egg and sugar mixture,
stirring constantly.

Pour mixture into four lightly greased ramekins (or tea cups).
Put ramekins into pan of water so that it comes at least halfway
up the sides.

Place the pan in a preheated 200°C oven. Bake for 15-20 minutes,
until a skin forms on the surface of the egg mixture. Remove from
the oven, allow to cool and then refrigerate for at least 5 hours –
or overnight. Sprinkle each top with a little sugar.

Put ramekins under a medium to hot grill, as close as possible to
the heat until the top is golden and crisp (about two minutes
should do it). Chill again and serve.

Guess Who's Succumbing to Dinner?

On the Richter scale of life's stresses, organising a dinner party has long been in the top ten. But if it does cause such distress, why do we do it at all?

What on earth has happened to the dinner party? Once a regular feature of any civilised social calendar, this ritual of polite society seems to be going the way of the dodo, the Rubik cube and the fondue set. Into obscurity.

Admittedly, on the Richter scale of life's stresses, organising a dinner party has long been in the top ten, coupled somewhere with moving house, losing one's job and receiving mail from the Deputy Commissioner of Taxation. But if it does cause such distress, why do we do it at all?

Is it because of our basic need to nurture or because we like to spoil people? Is it simply so that we can show off? Or is it masochism, pure and simple? Whatever the reason, as a society in the old days we used to do a lot of it.

In my late teens I would have a serious dinner party – by which I mean one where the food and the guests were both dressed for the occasion – at least twice a week. This is when candles would be brought out, flowers would be acquired from local parks, and wines would be French rather than Spanish.

The first of these I still remember with affection tinged with guilt.

It was London in the '60s, when the city 'swung like a pendulum do'. It was Carnaby Street, the mini skirt (first time round), white high-heeled boots, flares (first time round), and Twiggy. In those days Cream was what you had on the record player, Shrimp was a model, and joints were something you smoked (we never inhaled, of course.) Posters of Che Guevara hung on the walls. No-one walked anywhere, we marched as Joan Baez was exhorting us to overcome. And I was sharing a flat with two young women.

Despite its fancy Chelsea address, there was no bathroom, just the bath, which sat in the middle of the kitchen and had a door on it when it was not being used as a bath. It was our kitchen table. The problems of trying to prepare dinner with two elegant young women doing their ablutions in the same room can be imagined, I am sure.

On this occasion, between baths, I was cooking dinner for eight, mostly friends of my flatmates. I had prepared a main course of pork schnitzels with a mushroom and cream sauce, and planned to finish with the Belgian ice-cream classic, Dame Blanche (vanilla ice cream topped with hot chocolate sauce and nuts). A fairly rich collection of dishes but we were young and this was a '60s dinner party.

All went well until I discovered that all but one of the guests were strictly Jewish. To my later utter shame I renamed the main course veal schnitzel and served it to them, reasoning that if they had never eaten pork they would not know what it tasted like. 'Shame, shame' do I hear you cry? You are right. Doubtless I'll have to atone for my sin at some stage.

That dinner taught me things. First, planning is one of the most important pre-requisites for a successful meal, and second, a check on the dietary habits of your guests is a good idea. Another thing I learned was don't knock yourself out complicating the menu.

Recently a couple of friends invited me to a dinner party. It had been planned for weeks. Both good cooks with a passion for Italian food, they had spent two days on the preparations. On our arrival we guests were greeted by all four members of the family, the parents and their two boys, one aged three and the other 18 months old. We had canapes and champagne while the boys ran and crawled amok. Eventually the mother decided to leave the room to 'put the little one down'.

After 20 minutes or so – with more champagne, more canapes, and more amokery – the father decided that for our peace of mind it would be best to go and 'put the other one down', assuring us that he'd be back soon.

We didn't see them again. Three-quarters of an hour later we decided that the children and the cooking probably had taken their toll. We wrote them a note and went home.

Not all hosts have stress-related, work intensive dinner parties. Some are so laid back they don't prepare anything.

Friends I hadn't seen for some time had invited a few chums to their home in the country for dinner. On this wintry night, as the guests gathered round the wood stove in the large farmhouse kitchen to drink mulled wine and anticipate the meal ahead, the hostess – a lapsed city girl turned rural – pulled a large chicken out of the deep freeze, took off its plastic wrap, and put it with a slab of lard and a dozen whole, unpeeled potatoes into an electric frying pan.

"We're having chicken," she said, before pouring more mulled wine for us all.

"When?" I asked.

"Oh, how long do you think it will take? I thought about an hour," she responded with genuine enthusiasm.

Now there are those who would say I should have let matters take their course, however my hunger was getting the better of me, so I hijacked the bird, thawing it as quickly as I could by plunging it in cold water and as soon as was possible I removed the neck in its

Dinner party old-style: my birthday in Brussels.

plastic bag from the cavity, jointed the chicken, found some vegetables (also frozen) and set about knocking together a basic meal, which we ate about an hour later, by which time hosts and guests alike were well on the way to being under the table.

There has been at least one recorded case of dinner party-related suicide. That of French master cook Vatel (1635-71) who threw himself on his sword when a fish delivery failed to turn up. The fish came in a few minutes later.

It may pay to heed the words of British philanthropist Nubar Gulbenkian: "The best number for a dinner party is two: myself and a damn good head waiter."

Kate Lamont's Citrus Quinces

At her restaurant in Western Australia's Swan Valley, chef Kate Lamont uses wines produced at her parents' winery in several of her dishes. Although this recipe calls for quinces, it could also be made using firm pears.

Serves 6

INGREDIENTS

1 cup sugar

375 ml sweet white wine

seeds scraped from ½ vanilla
   pod (or ½ tsp vanilla
   essence)

2 lime leaves or 1 lemon leaf
   (optional)

1 cinnamon stick

grated rind and juice of:

   1 sweet grapefruit

   1 orange

   1 lemon

   1 lime

4 quinces

To serve

300ml natural yoghurt
   (thickened by straining
   through clean cotton or
   muslin for at least 4 hours)

1 tbsp honey

6-7 mint leaves, finely
   chopped

METHOD

Put sugar, wine, vanilla seeds and pod or essence, lime or lemon leaves (if using), cinnamon, and citrus juices and rinds in a non-reactive saucepan (such as stainless steel or glass) and bring to the boil to make a poaching syrup.

Peel quinces and cut into thick slices. Immediately put quinces into syrup to prevent discolouration. Poach quinces for at least 1 hour, or until they are tender.

Meanwhile, mix thickened yoghurt with honey.

Cool quinces, serve with yoghurt and garnish with mint.

Leftover potential: Keeps for two or three days in the refrigerator and may be served cold or reheated.

Hint: Low-fat yoghurt can be used.

Fruit Flamri

METHOD

Put water and wine in a heavy-based saucepan. Bring to the boil, then reduce heat and stirring constantly, sprinkle in semolina. Simmer over a low heat for 10 minutes, stirring occasionally. You should have a smooth mixture. If it dries out add a little more water – it doesn't matter if there are a few small lumps.

Beat egg yolks with caster sugar until sugar dissolves and the mixture is smooth.

Beat egg whites until stiff peaks form. Make sure that the mixing bowl and whisk are perfectly clean. Adding half a teaspoon cream of tartare will assist the process.

Transfer semolina to a mixing bowl. Stir in egg yolk mixture, then fold in beaten egg whites. Make sure they're not wildly mixed in – the mixture must remain aerated.

Drop dollops of mixture into greased ramekins or cups, cover lightly with plastic wrap and steam for 20 minutes. Allow flamris to cool a little before turning on to serving plates.

For berry sauce: Push berries through a fine sieve. Stir in icing sugar and strain again. If the berries taste too sweet, add a little lemon juice.

Serving suggestion: Serve warm or cold with the berry sauce and fruits of your choice.

Leftover potential: Keeps for two to three days in the refrigerator.

This is a terrific and simple recipe based on an old semolina pudding recipe. Semolina is simmered with dessert wine then sweetened, mixed with stiffly beaten egg whites and steamed to perfection.

Serves 6

INGREDIENTS

250ml water
250ml dessert wine (preferably a botrytis-affected riesling or semillon)
125g fine semolina
2 large egg yolks
2 tbsp caster sugar
2 large egg whites

Berry sauce
100g fresh or frozen raspberries (or other berries of your choice)
1 tbsp icing sugar

Tosia's Tipsy Pancakes

The best pancakes I have ever eaten were made by Tosia Kovacevic. Her pancakes are very thin, made with plain and self-raising flour, and a mixture of milk and water. I have often made them myself and while they always turn out well, they are never as perfect as Tosia's – and I'm furious!

Serves 6

INGREDIENTS

75g plain flour
75g self-raising flour
2 large eggs
125ml milk
125ml water
pinch salt
½ tsp vanilla essence
light flavoured oil for cooking
    (sunflower/canola)
strawberry jam (or other)
100g ground walnuts or
    pecans

Sauce

2 tbsp caster sugar
3 egg yolks
½ tsp vanilla essence
100ml sweet sherry
100ml cup port
100ml cream (optional)

METHOD

To make pancakes: Mix the pancake ingredients (flour, eggs, water, milk, salt, vanilla) without beating too much (it toughens the pancakes). Allow mixture to stand at least half an hour.

Cook pancakes in non-stick pan with a little oil smeared on bottom, piling them up and leaving in a warm place, until all the mixture has been used.

Spread each one with thin coating of jam, sprinkle with nuts and roll up each pancake before putting in a lightly oiled baking dish. Scatter remaining nuts on top.

To make sauce: Whisk sugar and egg yolks until the sugar has dissolved. Whisk in vanilla, sherry, port and cream (optional but it makes a richer dish).

Pour sauce over pancakes, cover with foil and bake in oven at 190°C for 30 minutes. Serve warm or cold.

Pineapple Spring Roll

Children love this tasty dessert which uses Australian canned pineapple, rolled with sultanas and almonds into a filo pastry parcel and baked to crisp perfection.

Serves 6

INGREDIENTS

1 tbsp custard powder (or cornflour)

1 x 200g can pineapple pieces, drained (reserving 2 tbsp juice from can)

1 tbsp caster sugar

50g sultanas

1 egg yolk

2 tbsp ground almond meal or chopped almonds

filo pastry

light tasting oil for brushing on pastry (canola, safflower or macadamia)

icing sugar for serving

METHOD

In a mixing bowl, combine custard powder (or cornflour) with reserved pineapple juice until a smooth mixture is obtained.

Put pineapple, sugar and sultanas into pan and bring to the boil. Quickly pour custard powder mixture into boiling fruit mixture, stirring vigorously. Remove from heat, stir in egg yolk and almonds, and allow to cool.

On lightly damp tea towel, lay out a sheet of filo pastry. Brush with a smear of oil. Place a dessertspoonful of pineapple mixture in the middle of nearside edge of pastry. Fold in sides. Roll up parcel. Place on lightly oiled baking tray.

Repeat process with rest of the mixture. When all parcels are on baking tray, brush with a little more oil.

Bake for 15-20 minutes in moderately hot oven (190°C) until golden brown.

To serve: Sprinkle with icing sugar.

Snow Eggs

A pavlova that's not baked but poached – extraordinary! Brian Ferguson, a contributor to Consuming Passions, *provides us with this stunningly simple delight. The French call it Oeufs à la Neige – I call it delicious.*

Serves 4

INGREDIENTS

2 fresh egg whites

2 tbsp pure icing sugar

1 cup fine caster sugar

2 cups skim milk

3ml vanilla essence

1 kiwi fruit, sliced

3-4 strawberries, sliced

pulp of 1 passionfruit

METHOD

Beat egg white (using an electric mixer will save time and energy) into stiff peaks.

Add pure icing sugar gently; this will strengthen the eggs, and they will not collapse when the heavier sugar is added. Continue to whisk.

Pour caster sugar onto a baking tray and spread out evenly. Place tray into oven preheated to 180°C for approximately 7 to 10 minutes or until the sugar has become hot on the surface, but not coloured as this will give the meringue an off-white shade.

Skim the hot surface of sugar with a spoon and add gently to the egg white, while continuing to beat.

When sugar is completely absorbed by the egg whites, the mixture should produce sharp stiff peaks, and have a nice shine.

Place a quarter cup of water into a saucepan; this will create a protective shield as the milk is added to the saucepan. Pour milk into saucepan and simmer. Add vanilla essence.

Scoop some of the egg white mixture out and, using two dessertspoons, form egg shapes. Place into the milk. Baste with milk mixture a few times then turn over and baste again; they will only take a few minutes to cook.

Gently scoop the poached snow eggs from the milk with a slotted spoon and place on a towel to drain.

To serve, arrange the snow eggs on to the dessert plates and decorate with the fresh fruit.

Summer Berry Pudding

A classically simple dessert using summer berries, bread – and vinegar. It's true, vinegar can enhance the flavour of berries. But only if it's good vinegar. A balsamic wine vinegar or a honey vinegar would be absolutely perfect!

Serves 6

METHOD

Put all ingredients except bread in large pan – preferably stainless steel or enamelled since the acid in the vinegar will react with some metals, such as aluminium.

Cook for two or three minutes until sugar has dissolved and the berries have rendered a good amount of juice.

Line a pudding basin or similar bowl with the bread slices, starting at the bottom and working outwards, making sure they overlap.

Add fruit to the bowl, slopping in plenty of juice which will soak into the bread. Pack the fruit down well. Just before you get to the top of the basin, stop adding fruit and cover with bread slices tucking the edges into the bowl.

Put plate on top of the bread and apply some weight (a house brick, for example). Place in refrigerator and leave overnight.

Strain remaining juice and reserve to pour over pudding.

Next day, remove weight and plate.

Using a knife, ease sides of the pudding away from the basin.

Put serving plate, bottom up, over the basin. Carefully, but quickly, turn over plate and basin so that the pudding may be released on to the serving plate. Cut into segments and serve.

INGREDIENTS

1 kg mixed berries
(strawberries, raspberries,
boysenberries, mulberries,
for example)
2 tsp mild vinegar (balsamic
or fruit vinegar)
2 strips lemon zest
1 cup raw sugar
1 tbsp orange or lemon jelly
crystals
12 or so slices white bread
with crusts removed (day
old bread is fine)

Hotel Survival Guide

Hotel brochures never contain glossy photos of rubbish bins, ventilation shafts and loading bays. This does not mean that they don't have them.

"What a great life you have, all that travel, all those luxury hotels..." It's a widely held belief that travel broadens the mind. In fact, more often than not, travel broadens one's prejudices. How often have I found myself stranded at airports, had luggage lost, been driven half crazy by piped music – to say nothing of the noisy rooms – been subjected to rude service. And paid a high price for the privilege.

It is not just room service, laundry services, restaurants and the mini-bar that can eat enormous holes in our budgets, we also are confronted with strange beds, unusual customs, and the requirement to listen to repeated mantras of "have a nice day", said with all the sincerity of a bank commercial.

I do spend much of my life in hotels – some the world's finest and others which make Fawlty Towers seem quite pleasant, but it has to be said that the worst of my experiences have been overseas, which is one of the reasons I mostly holiday in Australia and encourage others to do the same.

So if you are planning to be a hotel guest in the future, the following simple tips may help you achieve peace of body and mind.

Your room. Hotel brochures never contain glossy photos of rubbish bins, ventilation shafts and loading bays. This does not mean that they don't have them, or rooms overlooking them. They just don't want you to know they do – until you arrive. But these may

Travelling light. *Consuming Passions* crew on the road in search of more food experiences for the show.

be the views you get unless you get confirmation that your room overlooks the Sydney Opera House, the Taj Mahal, Torquay or whatever the hotel boasts.

If fresh air is important to you, make sure when you book that your windows can be opened. This may not be necessary if your hotel is next to a Bangkok waterway, but since properties tend to be overheated, underheated or a combination of both, access to the great outdoors can be helpful. **Room service** is a good form of dining, but it can have its pitfalls if you do not order carefully. For example, you are on the 64th floor of the hotel. The kitchen is in the basement. Once cooked, your meal may have to wait for an available waiter, especially in the peak hours. The waiter may bump into another waiter s/he hasn't seen for weeks, they chat for a few minutes and then s/he waits for a lift. It's probably best to order the salad.

The mini-bar trap. A Mars bar, box of macadamia nuts, or Pringles are foods you may not give much thought to most of the time. But try putting the thought behind you when you're trapped in a hotel room waiting for your dinner – which has now become supper. These goodies have become absolutely irresistible, as have the miniatures of spirits, even though they carry price tags close to your daily grocery bill.

One solution to avoid the mini-bar trap is to arrange for the hotel to empty the bar fridge before you arrive. Do not attempt this yourself. A travel journalist friend of mine staying at a very expensive hotel in Rome, removed the contents of the bar fridge and stocked it with his own provisions, mineral water, fresh fruit, juices, and yogurts. That night, returning to his room, he discovered the fridge had been restocked, leaving his goods, plus the ones he had removed, piled up nearby. Undeterred, he repeated the process twice, before he finally surrendered to management. It took quite a bit of lying on the floor in reception in the foetal position, and crying, before they agreed to remove the cost of three mini-bars worth of food and beverage from his account.

Restaurants in hotels are a danger zone. Self-catering can be a useful way of reducing the cost of a hotel stay, which is more easily done in Australia, where the practice is not discouraged. Most hotels in this country now provide kettles, some have toasters, and others have two useful catering tools: the iron and the hair dryer.

If you pack a roll of non-stick baking paper, a pastry brush and a little bottle of olive oil there is a tremendous amount of cooking you can do in your room. For instance, by brushing a thin fillet of fish or a veal escallop with a little oil and placing it between two sheets of baking paper, it can be ironed to perfection. Wool setting for rare, linen for well done.

Croissants or pies may be heated up, again using the perforated laundry bag. The pie is inserted, the hair dryer is placed in the bag's mouth and using the high setting the hot air blowing through the bag will heat the pie, and unlike using the microwave, the crust will not get soggy.

Prawns and other small seafoods may be cooked in electric kettles.

Toss some salad ingredients in the sink and before you know it you have a fabulous meal at a price you can afford.

And remember, the one good thing about bad hotels: the worse they are, the more you'll appreciate home when you get back.

Bon voyage.

> *It is because we put up with bad things that hotel keepers continue to give them to us.*
>
> **ANTHONY TROLLOPE** *novelist and traveller*

Fruit Baskets

These are a real treat. Puff pastry baskets holding fresh fruits sitting on top of pastry cream. Although in an ideal world freshly made puff pastry would be used, a bought pastry is quite adequate for this dessert.

Serves 4

INGREDIENTS

Fruit baskets

4 oven-friendly dessert dishes
    or large cups
aluminium foil
a little oil
4 puff pastry squares (approx.
    18cm x 18cm)
500g soft mixed fresh fruits,
    chopped (banana, paw
    paw, mango, berries, etc)
1 or 2 tbsp maple syrup

Pastry cream

3 egg yolks
4 tbsp caster sugar
1 tbsp cornflour
1 vanilla bean (or 2 tsp vanilla
    essence)
600ml reduced fat milk

METHOD

To make the fruit baskets: Turn the dessert dishes or cups upside down on a baking tray. Drape each with a square of aluminium foil. Rub the foil lightly with a little oil. Drape each dish or cup with a square of pastry.

Bake in a 180°C oven until the pastry case is golden brown. Remove from the oven, allow to cool. Remove the pastry case from the aluminium foil.

To make the pastry cream: Whisk the egg yolks with 2 tablespoons of sugar until smooth. Add cornflour and mix well.

If using vanilla bean, slit lengthwise, scrape out the seeds and place the seeds and the bean in the milk. Heat gently to boiling point along with the remaining sugar. (If using vanilla essence, add this now).

Once boiling, remove the bean, pour the milk into the egg yolk mixture. Whisk well. Pour into a milk pan, put it over a low heat and cook until the pastry cream is thick. Allow to cool.

When it's time to serve, put a dollop of pastry cream in each basket. Then top with the fresh fruits. Pour the maple syrup over the fruit.

Golden Pudding

Based on one of my mum's recipes, with some added tang.

Serves 6

INGREDIENTS

125g butter
100g caster sugar
2 large eggs, lightly beaten
grated rind of an orange
1 tbsp ginger (or other)
   marmalade
½ tsp cinnamon
150g self-raising flour
2 or 3 tbsp buttermilk
fresh orange slices
2 tbsp golden syrup
1 extra tbsp marmalade
25g unsalted butter
1 tbsp sugar
1 tbsp roasted hazelnuts
   (garnish)
natural yoghurt

METHOD

Cream the butter with the caster sugar to a smooth consistency.

Stir in the beaten eggs, grated orange rind, ginger marmalade, cinnamon and the flour.

Add the buttermilk and mix until you have a smooth thick batter.

In a large pudding basin, put enough orange slices to cover the bottom of the basin. Pour a mixture of the golden syrup and the extra marmalade over the orange slices. Add the pudding mixture.

Cover with non-stick baking paper, then a tea towel. Tie on to the basin. Immerse the basin in hot water in a saucepan so that the water comes halfway up the side of the basin.

Put the lid on the saucepan and allow the pudding to steam for one-and-a-half hours.

Meanwhile, caramelise some orange slices by tossing them in a mixture of butter and sugar over a medium heat for a few seconds.

Serving suggestion: Serve the pudding with the caramelised orange slices, roasted hazelnuts and yoghurt.

Mary's Marvellous Melange

Fine West Australian artist, Mary Moore is also an artist in the kitchen. This is another one of those recipes that are ideal for using up leftover pastries, but it's also worth buying the would-be leftovers just to make this extraordinary confection. It's hard to define because it's not really a tart, nor a pudding, nor a brioche, it's just a wonderful thing. Pastries are mixed with alcohol-plumped dried raisins, eggs, cream and almonds and then baked.

Serves 8

INGREDIENTS

500g leftover pastries
   (croissants, brioche,danish
   pastries, panettone)
7 medium eggs
150 caster sugar
600ml pouring cream
1 cup slivered almonds,
   toasted in dry pan
2 cups raisins, soaked in
   amaretto or brandy

METHOD

Break the pastries into bite-sized pieces in a large bowl. Whisk the eggs, sugar and cream until the sugar has dissolved.

Add the egg mixture, almonds and raisins to the pastries in the bowl and mix all the ingredients together.

Pour into a greased flan tin and bake at 180°C until set (approx. 1 hour).

Cover with baking paper or foil if it is browning too quickly.

Leftover potential: Best eaten the same day.

Mixed Nut Cake

This perfect dessert is an adaptation of a Lebanese recipe. A light, nutty cake served with a citrus sauce.

Serves 6-8

INGREDIENTS

1 cup biscuit crumbs
½ cup roughly chopped
    macadamia nuts
½ cup roughly chopped
    pecan nuts
100g sugar
4 large egg yolks
1 tsp vanilla essence
4 large egg whites
pinch of cream of tartar
icing sugar to garnish

Sauce
juice and segments of 1
    grapefruit and 1 orange
500ml orange juice
2 tsp citrus peel
1 cinnamon stick
1 tbsp orange marmalade
1 tbsp sugar
2 tsp almond or kirsch liqueur
    (optional)

METHOD

To make the sauce: Make the sauce first. Mix the citrus fruit, juice and the peel with the cinnamon, marmalade and sugar in a non-stick pan. Cook over a low heat until it has reduced to a thick syrup (about 25 minutes). Set aside and keep warm.

To make the cake: Mix the biscuit crumbs and nuts together. Beat the sugar with the egg yolks and vanilla until the sugar has dissolved.

Whisk the egg whites with cream of tartar until peaks form. Slowly fold the egg yolk mixture and the nut and biscuit mixture into the egg whites.

Pour into a high-sided cake or bread tin lined with non-stick baking paper (or use a non-stick baking tin). Bake at 180°C for 30 to 40 minutes.

When it's time to serve, stir the liqueur (if using) through the sauce. Cut the cake into segments, and serve with the sauce. Sprinkle with icing sugar.

Apple Cobbler

This cobbler originated in America's Deep South and has nothing to do with fish or shoe repairs. It's a dessert like a pie but much easier to make.

Serves 6

INGREDIENTS

zest and juice of 1 lemon
3 large granny smith apples,
    roughly chopped
2 tsp cornflour
1 tsp cinnamon
$\frac{1}{2}$ tsp powdered cloves
2 tbsp raw or brown sugar
1 small can peach slices,
    drained

Topping
1 cup flour
2 tsp baking powder
1 tbsp butter
$\frac{1}{2}$ cup milk

Crème Anglaise
2 egg yolks
1 tbsp caster sugar
$\frac{1}{2}$ tsp vanilla
1 tsp cornflour
1 cup milk

METHOD

Into a large mixing bowl place lemon zest and juice, and chopped apple. Toss together. Add cornflour, cinnamon, cloves and sugar and mix together well. Put into baking dish and place the peaches on top.

To make topping: In a separate bowl crumble together flour, baking powder and butter until light, then add the milk and mix to a light dough.

Preheat oven to 190°C. Roll small amounts of the dough into balls and flatten, then place on top of fruit mix. Sprinkle with sugar and place in the oven. Bake for 40 minutes.

To make Crème Anglaise: Mix the egg yolks, caster sugar, vanilla and cornflour until creamy. Now add a cup of boiling milk and mix thoroughly. Put this mixture into the saucepan and cook over low heat (it must not boil) until it has thickened.

Serve the cobbler hot or cold with Crème Anglaise.

Mauritian Coconut-filled Pancakes

This is a superb dessert from Jean-Claude Michel executive chef at the Shandrani Hotel on Mauritius. It is especially fine when made with freshly grated coconut, whole vanilla beans and Mauritian rum. It may also be made with dry shredded coconut, vanilla essence and Australian rum.

Serves 8

INGREDIENTS

750ml full-cream milk

3 vanilla beans, split
    lengthwise (or 1 tsp vanilla
    essence)

100g raisins

500g freshly grated coconut
    (or 250g dried coconut)

2 tbsp sugar

2 tbsp rum (preferably
    Mauritian)

8 cooked pancakes

METHOD

Put milk into a saucepan and bring to the boil. Reduce heat, add vanilla beans, raisins, coconut, sugar and rum. If using vanilla essence, add at this time. Simmer slowly for 10 minutes. Strain and reserve the liquid.

Put a little coconut mixture on the edge of a pancake, roll up and place in greased baking dish. Repeat until all pancakes are filled and packed into the dish.

Spoon over any remaining coconut mixture, then pour over reserved liquid and bake at 190°C for 10 minutes.

Leftover potential: Poor, eat immediately.

Pears in Dessert Wine Sauce

Impress your dinner guests with this ridiculously easy dessert combining canned pears with a warm white wine sauce, served with a contrastingly cold vanilla ice-cream and topped with a crunchy almond praline. I find the dish is best made with an Australian botrytis-affected semillon or riesling (a so-called sticky) wine, but any good fruity white wine will do.

Serves 4

INGREDIENTS

250ml orange juice
juice and rind of 1 lemon
1 tbsp sugar
250ml dessert wine
1 cinnamon stick
2 or 3 cloves
8 halves of canned Australian
    pears, drained and juice or
    syrup reserved
low-fat vanilla ice cream,
    to serve

Praline

75g unblanched almonds
75g caster sugar

METHOD

Put orange juice, lemon juice and rind, sugar, wine, cinnamon stick, cloves and reserved pear juice in a non-reactive saucepan and cook over medium heat for about 15 minutes, or until reduced to one-quarter of its original volume, and a delicious syrup has formed.

To make praline: Put almonds and sugar in a heavy-based saucepan and cook over low heat, stirring, until sugar melts. Continue cooking over low heat until syrup is golden. Pour mixture on to an oiled baking tray and allow to set. Place praline in food processor and process to crush. Alternately, you can place the praline between sheets of baking paper and crush with a rolling pin.

To serve: Pour a puddle of syrup on to each serving plate. Place a dollop of ice-cream in the centre and stand the pear halves on either side. Sprinkle with a little praline.

Leftover potential: Cooked pears will keep in the refrigerator for two to three days. Praline keeps almost indefinitely in an airtight container.

Yoghurt Honey Ice

A low-fat ice-cream recipe given to me by Canadian chef Roger Dufaut. Particularly good when made with Tasmania's incomparable leatherwood honey. The recipe involves using buttermilk which, despite its name, is low in fat, as it is the by-product of butter manufacture.

Serves 8

INGREDIENTS

500g natural low fat yoghurt

250g buttermilk

4 tbsp honey

2 tsp grated lemon rind

2 tbsp grated orange rind

2 tbsp orange juice

2 tbsp lemon juice

1 egg white beaten to soft
  peak stage

METHOD

Mix ingredients in the order given, except the egg white.

Put mixture in ice-cream maker and churn until mixture starts to firm. Mix in egg white and continue churning until the ice-cream has set.

Note: If you do not possess an ice-cream maker, this ice-cream may be made in the deep freeze. Put in mixing bowl and remove from freezer every 10 minutes to prevent ice crystals from forming.

Remains of the Day

I share my mother's passion for leftovers. I love using them up to make new dishes, which in turn become leftovers. I love the continuum.

my wife does great things with leftovers – she throws them away," a friend once told me. What a tragedy, I thought.

Leftovers have played such an important part in my life since I was knee high to the fridge door, so much so that often they gave me greater pleasure than the dish did in its original state.

My mother, it has to be said, is the Queen of the Leftover and I know that's where my enthusiasm comes from.

With this fervent conservationist parent, nothing ever goes to waste. Whether it's cold baked potatoes, meat from the roast, or pre-loved cabbage, it gets incorporated into a new concoction. Cooked fish could become patties. In a trice, stale cake goes into a trifle. Gravy goes into a batch of stock.

She's very clever, my mum.

Anticipating a visit from me, she will deliberately cook too much food in the preceding days knowing that on my arrival the first thing I will do is to pay a visit to the fridge.

It would not be unusual to encounter a small dish bearing a half sausage and a dozen or so baked beans left over from an earlier breakfast.

And there would always be dishes of mashed potatoes and brussels sprouts ready to be turned into that uniquely British creation, bubble-and-squeak. Being a chip off the old block, I now share her passion. I love using up leftovers to make new dishes, which in turn become leftovers. I love the continuum.

It could be a lamb and sweet potato curry which started life as a lamb roast. Roast pumpkin may well finish up in a risotto. A soup may be boiled up with additional herbs and vegetables, strained, cleared with egg white and transformed into a stock. Cold cooked poultry meat need only be diced and tossed in a pan with onion, garlic, cooked rice and a little salt and pepper to become a delightful pilaf.

Leftover carrots and peas can be mixed with mayonnaise, chives and hard boiled egg to become a tasty salad.

And of course any remnants of cooked pasta only need to be tossed with some extra virgin olive oil, good vinegar, slices of tomato and slivers of parmesan or pecorino to make a fabulous light lunch.

Bread can be dried and made into breadcrumbs, remembering that if it is not fully dry, it will go mouldy within a few days, even in an airtight container. Or it could be made into a traditional Mediterranean stale bread salad. Stale croissants and Danish pastries may be mixed with raisins, cream, eggs and re-baked.

Vintage lasagna may be cheered up by breaking it up in the baking dish and warming it, making a little fresh cheese sauce, pouring it over the warmed lasagna and putting the dish under the grill for a few minutes.

Naturally, there is the danger of too many cooks spoiling the broth, as in the Case of the Scouts Farewell Camp Fire Dinner. I had been invited to join a large and enthusiastic scout troop to celebrate the last night of a camping expedition. Gathered round a roaring fire were roaring young people busily tossing foods into a large cauldron with great gusto. Keen not to leave anything behind them but their footprints, everything that was left at the camp went into a most alarming curry.

A medley of canned steak and onions, potatoes, instant potato, peas, canned corn and pineapple, was joined by large quantities of sultanas, tomato soup and last – but certainly not least – a jar of maraschino cocktail cherries, with heavy syrup! What a tribute to the imagination of these young men in uniform. It finished up tasting like a cross between an Irish stew and a rich fruit cake, but refusal would certainly have caused offence.

For the true devotee of the leftover, there is no better time than Christmas time, when the fridge is likely to be bulging with ham, turkey, pork, nuts and Christmas pudding. But it can be a year-round pleasure.

Next time you are planning to throw something into the composter, think about giving it a new lease of life.

Even an old boot tastes good if it is cooked over charcoal.

ANONYMOUS *Italian Proverb*

Weights and Measures

METRIC CUPS AND SPOON SIZES

Cup
1/4 cup = 60ml
1/3 cup = 80ml
1/2 cup = 125ml
1 cup = 250ml

Spoon*
1/4 teaspoon = 1.25ml
1/2 teaspoon = 2.5ml
1 teaspoon = 5ml
1 tablespoon = 20ml

*Note: In this book teaspoon is abbreviated to tsp and tablespoon to tbsp.

OVEN TEMPERATURES

	Fahrenheit	Celsius
Very Slow	250°	120°
Slow	275-300°	140-150°
Moderately Slow	325°	160°
Moderate	350°	180°
Moderately Hot	375°	190°
Hot	400-450°	200-230°
Very Hot	475-500°	250-260°

MASS (WEIGHT)

Imperial	Metric
1/2oz	15g
1oz	30g
2oz	60g
3oz	90g
4oz (1/4lb)	125g
5oz	155g
6oz	185g
7oz	220g
8oz (1/2lb)	250g
9oz	280g
10oz	315g
11oz	345g
12oz (3/4lb)	375g
13oz	410g
14oz	440g
15oz	470g
16oz (1lb)	500g (0.5kg)
24oz (1 1/2lb)	750g
32oz (2lb)	1000g (1kg)

LENGTH

Inches	Centimetres
1/4	0.5
1/2	1
3/4	2
1	2.5
1 1/2	4
2	5
2 1/2	6
3	8
4	10
6	15
7	18
8	20
9	23
10	25
12	30
14	35
16	40
18	45
20	50

LIQUIDS

Imperial	Cup*	Metric
1 fl oz		30ml
2 fl oz	1/4	60ml
3 fl oz		100ml
4 fl oz	1/2	125ml
5 fl oz		150ml
6 fl oz	3/4	200ml
8 fl oz	1	250ml
10 fl oz (1/2 pint)	1 1/4 cups	300ml
12 fl oz	1 1/2 cups	375ml
14 fl oz	1 3/4 cups	425ml
15 fl oz		475ml
16 fl oz	2 cups	500ml
20 fl oz (1 pint)	2 1/2 cups	600ml

*Note: Cup measures are the same in Imperial and Metric.

Index